THE BOOK OF
REVELATION

THE BOOK OF
REVELATION

RANKO STEFANOVIC

Pacific Press®
Publishing Association
Nampa, Idaho | Oshawa, Ontario, Canada
www.pacificpress.com

Cover design resources from Lars Justinen

Copyright © 2018 by Pacific Press® Publishing Association
Printed in the United States of America
All rights reserved

Adapted from *Plain Revelation* (Berrien Springs, MI: Andrews University Press, 2013).

The author assumes full responsibility for the accuracy of all facts and quotations as cited in this book.

Scripture quotations from Revelation are the author's translation.

Scripture quotations marked KJV are from the King James Version of the Bible.

Scripture quotations marked NASB are taken from the NEW AMERICAN STANDARD BIBLE®, copyright © 1960, 1962, 1963, 1968, 1971, 1972, 1973, 1975, 1977, 1995 by The Lockman Foundation. Used by permission. www.lockman.org

Scripture quotations marked RSV are from the Revised Standard Version of the Bible, copyright © 1946, 1952, and 1971 by the Division of Christian Education of the National Council of the Churches of Christ in the United States of America. Used by permission. All rights reserved.

Additional copies of this book are available for purchase by calling toll-free 1-800-765-6955 or by visiting http://www.adventistbookcenter.com.

ISBN: 978-0-8163-6382-7

June 2018

It's all about Jesus 🙂

Contents

Introduction

Of all the books in the Bible, Revelation has drawn the most interest and curiosity. Yet, for many Christians, its contents remain a mystery. Ironically, the book entitled "Apocalypse" (meaning "revelation" or "unveiling") has become a symbol of confusion and obscurity. Many have not bothered with it because of the strange images and frightening scenes it describes.

But Revelation clearly shows it was written to be understood (Revelation 22:10). The beginning of the book states, "Blessed is the one who reads and the ones listening" (Revelation 1:3), describing a public reading of the book. Great blessings are promised to all who read its pages, heed its messages, and treasure them in their minds and hearts (Revelation 22:7). To unlock the meaning of this important book, some basic principles of prophetic interpretation, which are listed below, will guide our study.

Interpretative approaches to Revelation

No book of the Bible has been the object of so many interpretative approaches as Revelation. The question of how to interpret and apply its prophecies has generated plenty of debate in the last several centuries. Today, there are four distinctive interpretative approaches to the book.

Preterism. *Preterism* (from the Latin *praeter*, meaning "past") is a method of interpretation that places the whole significance of Revelation in the past, specifically with the Christian church in Asia Minor and its struggle with Rome at that time. In this view, Revelation does not predict the future but was intended to encourage Christians of John's day to persevere in their faithfulness to God.

Futurism. In contrast to preterism, *futurism* exclusively interprets the prophecies of Revelation from the end-time perspective. Futurist interpreters hold that Revelation 4–22 will be fulfilled shortly, before the second coming of Christ. Futurism interprets the symbols of Revelation as literally as possible. Today, this is the preferred method of most Protestant Evangelicals.

Idealist. The idealist approach is based on preterist ideas. It recognizes that Revelation describes what was happening to Christians in the first century. But idealist interpreters contend that the book describes, in vivid symbolism, the ongoing struggle between good and evil that will result in God's ultimate triumph over evil. The book does not speak about literal events fulfilled in the past or the future from our temporal perspective. The messages of Revelation provide general guidance to Christians of every generation.

Historicist. The historicist approach to prophetic interpretation believes Revelation portrays, in symbolic presentations, the course of history unfolding from the first century until the end time. Some prophecies of the book were fulfilled in the past, some are yet to be fulfilled, and some refer to the present time. The events themselves are real; however, they are portrayed in symbolic language. Historicism was the method of prophetic interpretation used by Protestants until the nineteenth century.

In evaluating these approaches, one notices that preterism limits the relevance of Revelation's messages to the first-century Christians. Similarly, futurism limits the prophecies of Revelation exclusively to the last generation of Christians. These two methods seem deficient, because they imply that Revelation has nothing to offer the generations between John's time and the time of the end. Revelation plainly shows that the first three chapters concern John's time (see Revelation 1:11). But Revelation 4:1 states that the rest of the book (chaps. 4–22) deals with events that will take place beyond John's time and continue until the time of the end.

A major problem with preterism and idealism is their denial of the book's predictive prophecies. Revelation claims to be a book of prophecy (Revelation 1:3; 22:7, 10). John clearly states, both in the introduction and the conclusion of the book, that its purpose is to show God's people events that take place in the future (Revelation 1:1; 22:6). Any interpretative method that denies the predictive nature of Revelation does not do justice to the obvious claims of the book. Both preterism and idealism fail on this ground.

These issues leave historicism as the only adequate approach for prophetic interpretation. Historicism sees the events predicted in Revelation as taking place both in the past and the future as well as in the centuries that lie between. This method also recognizes the spiritual applications of the book's messages. This inclusive approach makes it reasonable to conclude that the historicist interpretation does the best job of discovering the relevance of Revelation's messages for all generations, even until the end of the age.

Sanctuary structure

The structure of Revelation is also closely linked with the sanctuary services in the Old Testament, replete with references to the temple and its articles of furniture. In this structure, Revelation falls into seven major divisions reflecting the daily and annual services of the earthly sanctuary. Each of these parts is introduced with a sanctuary scene.

The sequence of these introductory sanctuary scenes reveals a line of progression in the heavenly sanctuary that starts with the inauguration of Christ as the High Priest. He then ascends to His heavenly throne where the sanctuary phases continue; intercession, judgment, the close of intercession, and the absence of priestly activities. The sequence concludes with God joining His people in the New Jerusalem.

The structure of Revelation, based on the sanctuary's daily and yearly patterns, helps us to locate the key visions of the book within their historical context. First, it points to Revelation 11:19 as a dividing line between the historical and end-time sections of the book. While the first half of Revelation focuses primarily on the Christian age, the second half focuses exclusively on the end time after Christ's mediatory ministry comes to a close. It shows that the visions of the seven seals and the seven trumpets run throughout Christian history, while the seven last plagues take place exclusively at the time of the end.

Threefold structure

Apart from the prologue (Revelation 1:1–8) and the epilogue (Revelation 22:6–21), the main body of Revelation falls into three distinctive parts: (a) the messages to the seven churches, which primarily focus on the historical situation within these churches in Asia Minor during John's time (Revelation 1:9–3:22); (b) the historical section, which primarily focuses on history's unfolding from the first century until the end of time (Revelation 4–11); and (c) the eschatological section, which primarily focuses on the time of the end and the events leading up to the coming of Christ and the establishment of God's kingdom (Revelation 12:1–22:5). These divisions are related to the three periods of history within the book's perspective: the time of John, the Christian age, and the end time.

It is especially significant that each of these three divisions begins with a special vision of Jesus Christ. In each of these introductory visions, Jesus is presented in a unique role. His portrayal in these visions defines the theological perspective of the subsequent scenes and affirms that the last book of the Bible is truly a revelation of Jesus Christ.

Recognizing the importance of a structure based on the daily and annual sanctuary services, the exposition of Revelation in this book follows this threefold structure. I urge you to put aside any preconceived ideas and allow the book to speak to you. A proper understanding of Revelation's messages will move us to search our souls and confidently prepare for the future. "Blessed is the one who heeds the words of the prophecy of this book" (Revelation 22:7).

The Gospel From Patmos

Revelation begins with a prologue (verses 1–8) that provide some introductory information about the book including the author, the recipients, the book's central theme, the purpose of the book, and how it was written. It also introduces the key theme of the book.

The central theme of Revelation (1:1a)

The book begins with the opening statement "the revelation of Jesus Christ." This declaration generates the title of the book, calling it "the revelation of Jesus Christ." The Greek word *apokalupsis* (apocalypse) means "unveiling," "uncovering," or "revealing." The Apocalypse is, thus, an unveiling of Jesus Christ.

In the original language, the phrase "a revelation of Jesus Christ" may mean either that the revelation is from Jesus or that it is about Jesus as the One revealed. In a sense, both meanings are implied here. While the revelation came from God through Jesus Christ, who communicated it to John through an angel (Revelation 1:1; cf. Revelation 22:16), the rest of the book testifies that Jesus is the main subject of its contents. He is "the Alpha and the Omega" (that is, the A to Z) of the book's content, "the beginning and the end" (Revelation

21:6; 22:13), and "the first and the last" (Revelation 1:17; 22:13). The book begins and concludes with Jesus.

The book of Revelation is a gospel as much as the four Gospels are. Like the Gospels, Revelation talks about the same Jesus. But they focus on different aspects of His roles and existence. The Gospels portray Jesus as the preexistent Son of God who entered into human experience to save fallen human beings and who, after His death on the cross and subsequent resurrection, ascended to heaven. What is He now doing in heaven? Revelation unveils the answer to this question. The book reveals that after His ascension to heaven, Jesus was seated on the heavenly throne, ruling over the entire universe.

The Gospels also tell us that before His ascension, Jesus made two promises about His future interactions with His people: first, He will always be with them, until the time of the end (Matthew 28:20); and second, He will come again to take them to Himself (John 14:1–3). Revelation picks up on these two promises and describes, first, how Jesus fulfills the promise to be with His people throughout history, even to the end (Revelation 1–18), and second, how He will come at the conclusion of this world's history and be united with them (Revelation 19–22).

Without Revelation, our knowledge of Christ's ministry in heaven on behalf of His people would be vague. Revelation conveys the substance of the gospel as "the good news" and emphatically points to the glorified Christ as the One who, by virtue of His own death, conquered death and the grave (Revelation 1:17, 18). He will never forsake His people and will always be with them until He comes the second time to take them home.

Purpose of the book (1:1b)

The prologue further states that the purpose of Revelation is to show God's people "the things which must soon take place" (Revelation 1:1). It is obvious that the portrayal of future events occupies much of the book. While the first half of Revelation (chaps. 1–11) delineates worldwide events that take place between the first century and the time of the end, its second half (chaps. 12–22) deals primarily with the time of the end and events leading to the Second Coming. This division suggests a question: How can the book be both the unveiling of Jesus Christ and the unveiling of events that will take place?

For one, the prophecies of Revelation explain, from God's perspective, why the predicted events will happen. They provide assurance that no matter what the future brings, God is in control. But the future events predicted in Revelation are evidently not the primary theme. They are not recorded to make the Apocalypse a divine fortune-telling book nor are the prophecies given to satisfy our obsessive curiosity about the future. Their primary purpose is to assure us of Jesus' presence with His people throughout history and its final events.

Christ knew, however, that the full impact of His promise to be with His people would not be effective without unpacking future events through His prophetic word. The graphic portrayal of these events in His message is designed to impress on us the gravity of the final crisis and our need to depend on God during this time. This time of crisis will remind God's people of Christ's promise to be with them in order to sustain them during difficult times. "These things I have spoken to you," Jesus said, "so that when their hour comes, you may remember that I told you of them" (John 16:4, NASB).

We must keep in mind that the fulfillment of end-time prophecies must not be a subject of speculation and sensationalism. Revelation informs us about events at the time of the end, but what it does not reveal is exactly when and how they will take place. Numerous books and websites have predicted exactly how these prophecies will be fulfilled, but most of the ideas expressed are misleading. They are drawn not from the Bible but rather from imaginings based on allegorical interpretations or headline news. The timing and manner of the unfolding of the final events are God's secrets and reserved only for Himself (Matthew 24:36; Acts 1:7). They will be clear to us only when they are fulfilled, not before (John 14:29; 16:4).

When understood properly, the prophecies of Revelation serve practical purposes: to teach us how to live today and to prepare us for the future. Studying them should make us better people, motivate us to take our destinies seriously, and inspire us to try to reach others with the gospel message.

Symbolic language of the book (1:1c)

The prologue further explains that the contents of Revelation were "signified" to John in a vision. The Greek word *sémainó* (signify) carries the primary meaning "to show by signs or symbols." This word is used in the Greek translation of the Old Testament (the Septuagint) where Daniel explained to King Nebuchadnezzar that by means of a symbol God had shown to the king "what will take place in the future" (Daniel 2:45, NASB). Similarly, by employing this word in the prologue of Revelation, John informs the reader that the things recorded in the book are visions and symbols that were shown to him on Patmos.

The book of Revelation does not provide photographic descriptions of heavenly realities or future events that should be interpreted literally. Although the scenes and events predicted are real, they were shown to John in symbolic presentations. Under the inspiration of the Holy Spirit, John faithfully recorded these symbolic presentations exactly as they were shown to him (Revelation 1:2). But due to the inadequacy of human language, John added symbols of his own. His attempts at putting heavenly realities in human words are identified by marker words such as *like* and *as*.

Keeping the symbolic character of Revelation in mind will safeguard against the literal application of symbols, which could distort the prophetic message. While reading the Bible in general presupposes a literal understanding of the text (unless it clearly points to intended symbolism), studying Revelation calls for a symbolic understanding of the scenes and events recorded, unless the text clearly indicates that a literal meaning is intended.

The symbolic language of Revelation was not born in a

vacuum but was drawn from historical reality. Most of the symbolism in the book was taken from the Old Testament: some three-fourths of the book's text has direct or indirect allusions to the Old Testament. In portraying future events, Inspiration often uses the language of the past. God wants to impress upon our minds that His acts of salvation in the future will be much like His acts of salvation in the past. What He did for His people in the past, He will do for them in the future. There is no doubt that first-century readers of Revelation would have understood most of the symbols in Revelation in light of their Old Testament background.

Thus, in unlocking the meaning of the symbols and images in Revelation, we must first pay attention to the Old Testament. Many symbols in the book were also widely used in Jewish apocalyptic writings of the time. As such, they were part of people's vocabulary in the first century. Additionally, Revelation's images would have also evoked contemporary Greco-Roman scenes in the minds of first-century Christians.

The Trinitarian greeting (1:4-6)

Revelation was originally written in the form of an epistle. As such, it starts with the threefold opening of letters that was customary at the time. First, it introduces the sender and the recipients of the letter: "John to the seven churches that are in Asia" (Revelation 1:4). John was one of the twelve disciples and the writer of the Gospel that bore his name. He was writing to seven Christian congregations in the Roman province of Asia (now the southwestern part of Turkey), which were mired in dire spiritual circumstances.

In Revelation, those seven churches represent the church throughout the Christian age. Seven is the number of fullness and completeness; although originally written to those seven churches, Revelation was thus also written for all God's people throughout the Christian age.

The second part of the letter's opening gives the common epistolary greeting among the early Christians: "Grace and peace to you" (verse 4; cf. Romans 1:7; 1 Peter 1:2). The phrase consists of the customary Greek greeting word *charis* (grace) and the Hebrew greeting word *shalom* (peace). In the New Testament, "grace and peace" is more than just a casual greeting. The order of these two words is always "grace and peace," never "peace and grace."[1] Robert H. Mounce points out that this is because "grace is the divine favor" bestowed upon human beings and "peace is that state of spiritual well-being that follows as a result."[2]

The givers of grace and peace are the Three Persons of the Godhead. The first mentioned is God the Father, referred to as "the One who is, and who was, and who is coming" (Revelation 1:4; cf. Revelation 4:8). This tripartite title echoes the divine name "I am who I am," which interpreted the Old Testament covenant name *Yahweh* and pointed to God's eternal existence (Exodus 3:14, NASB).

The Second Person in the Trinity is called "the seven Spirits" (Revelation 1:4; cf. Revelation 4:5; 5:6). This name refers to the Holy Spirit, with seven being a number of fullness. The Old Testament background of this identification is the sevenfold designation of the Spirit, found in the Septuagint version of Isaiah 11:2, 3.[3] In Zechariah 4, the seven lamps symbolize the universal activity of the Holy Spirit in the world (verse 2). In Revelation, "the seven Spirits" parallel the seven churches in which the Spirit operates. The phrase represents the fullness and universality of the Holy Spirit's work in the church, enabling the church to fulfill its calling.

The list concludes with Jesus Christ, who is identified with a threefold title: "The faithful witness, the firstborn from the dead, and the ruler of the kings of the earth" (Revelation 1:5a). This threefold title echoes Psalm 89, in which the Davidic king is the firstborn of Yahweh, the exalted king on earth, and the faithful witness for Yahweh (Psalm 89:27, 37). These three titles of Jesus in Revelation 1:5a correspond to His titles of Prophet, Priest, and King. By virtue of His faithful witness during His earthly sojourn, Jesus has received the honor of the firstborn and has been exalted to the highest rank, above all powers and authority in heaven and on earth (Ephesians 1:20–22; 1 Peter 3:22).

Having stated Jesus' true identity, John then describes what Jesus does (Revelation 1:5b, 6). This threefold activity corresponds to His three titles. In the original text, "[He] loves us" is an ongoing activity: He loves us continually. This love embraces equally the past, the present, and the future. The One who loves us has loosed us from our sins by His blood. In the original text, the verb "loosed" refers to the completed act in the past. On the cross, Jesus died and released us from our sins forever.

Revelation tells us not only what Christ has done for us but also what we may become in Him. He has made us "a kingdom, priests to His God and Father" (verse 6; cf. Revelation 5:9, 10). The redeemed enjoy this status because of what Christ did on the cross of Calvary. This status, originally promised to ancient Israel, was realized in their redemption from the slavery of Egypt and the promise that they would be His kingdom of priests (Exodus 19:5, 6). This privileged title is now offered to the Christian church as the true Israel of God (1 Peter 2:9, 10). What was offered to Israel as a future promise, is now offered to Christians based on what Christ did in the past.

The keynote of the book (1:7, 8)

In concluding the prologue, John directs attention to the keynote of the letter: the return of Jesus in majesty and glory. He employs wording from Daniel 7:13 (coming with the clouds) and Zechariah 12:10 (whom they have pierced and they will mourn for Him) as well as the words of Matthew 24:30 from Jesus' Olivet discourse (coming on the clouds of the sky and all the tribes of the earth will mourn). John wants us to understand that Christ's coming is rooted in biblical prophecy and in Christ's promise to come again.

In the New Testament, Christ always refers to His coming with the words "I am coming" rather than "I will come." The futuristic present tense refers to the future event as already occurring, thus demonstrating the certainty of Christ's promise to come again. This certainty is affirmed with the statement "Yes, amen" (Revelation 1:7). In Greek, it reads as *"Nai*, amen."

Nai is a Greek word that means "amen," which is a Hebrew affirmative. When combined, the two words express an emphatic affirmation. This affirmation also concludes the book: " 'Yes, I am coming soon.' Amen. Come, Lord Jesus" (Revelation 22:20).

This text refers to the literal and personal coming of Christ in majesty and glory. In this way, Revelation is in line with the teaching of the rest of the Bible. Nowhere in the Bible does it teach an invisible and secret coming of Christ. On the contrary, every human will witness Him coming, and this includes "those who pierced Him" (Revelation 1:7). Nobody will be exempt. While His coming brings deliverance to those waiting for Him, it will bring judgment to those who have spurned His mercy and love.

The certainty of the Second Coming is rooted in the fact that it has been promised by God Himself, the great "I AM," who is "the Alpha and the Omega . . . the One who is, and who was, and who is coming, the Almighty" (Revelation 1:8). A promise is as strong as the person giving the promise. It is as certain as the integrity and ability of the person to do what he or she says. In the Bible, the promise to come again is given by the God of the universe—a God who has always kept His promises.

---

1. Bruce M. Metzger, *Breaking the Code: Understanding the Book of Revelation* (Nashville, TN: Abingdon Press, 1993), 23.

2. Robert H. Mounce, *The Book of Revelation*, New International Commentary on the New Testament (Grand Rapids, MI: Eerdmans, 1977), 68.

3. Lancelot C. L. Brenton, trans., *The Septuagint With Apocrypha: Greek and English* (Peabody, MA: Hendrickson, 1986).

CHAPTER

Among the Lampstands

John on Patmos (1:9)

In this section, John describes the circumstances in which he received the visions of Revelation and his visionary encounter with the glorified Christ. John begins his story by saying he was on Patmos because of his faithful witness to the gospel (Revelation 1:9). Early Christian authors are unanimous that John was banished to this rocky and barren island by Roman authorities to prevent him from spreading the gospel. As a prisoner, the aged apostle endured many hardships in his exile on Patmos. Early Christian tradition testifies that he was forced to perform hard labor in quarries.[1]

John's experience on Patmos shaped the language and imagery of Revelation. For instance, the tribulation that he endured because of his faithful witness to the gospel became a precursor of the faithful people's experience in a hostile world but especially of the great tribulation God's people will have to go through at the time of the end (cf. Revelation 7:14). Also, John probably had the mountainous island of Patmos in mind when he mentioned the islands and mountains disappearing at the end of time (Revelation 6:14; 16:20).

Especially noticeable is the prominence of sea and water imagery in the book (occurring twenty-six times). Since John was confined to Patmos, the sea also came to mean separation and suffering to him. The stormy waters around the island came to symbolize the disturbing social and political conditions in the world. The sea is obviously related to the *abussos* (bottomless pit), which is the abode of Satan and his demons (cf. Revelation 13:1 with 17:8). It is out of that metaphoric sea that the apostle saw the beast coming to oppress God's people (Revelation 13:1). The prostitute Babylon was seen as dwelling "on many waters" (Revelation 17:1; cf. verse 15). It is also from the symbolic sea that the figurative merchants of Babylon, selling their corrupt doctrines and policies, get all their wealth and luxuries (Revelation 18:17–24).

With this in mind, it is no wonder that in John's last vision of the new heaven and the new earth he first observed that "the sea is no longer there" (Revelation 21:1). The text does not refer to just any sea but to *the* sea that surrounded Patmos, filling the aged apostle with a deep longing for the time when the sea will be no longer. The absence of the "sea" on the new earth means the absence of all evil and the "Patmos" of suffering and pain in daily life.

The real pain, however, that the revelator felt on Patmos was greater than his physical suffering. He was overwhelmingly concerned with the situation in the churches, located in seven cities in the province of Asia (cf. Revelation 1:11), that had been deprived of his leadership. The situation in the churches gradually destabilized because of the increasing hostility of the Roman authorities toward Christians in Asia. There were also disturbing reports that these churches were in crisis. Most of them were divided; in some, the majority of believers were involved in spreading apostasy.

Many Christians in Asia were struggling with regard to their identity. The dire circumstances and distress might have led many of them to question whether God was still in control and what the future would bring for the church. They were in urgent need of guidance and encouragement. But the aged apostle could not be with them. His concern for their spiritual welfare was, at times, overwhelming. John was in great distress and needed a word of assurance and encouragement.

Christians should never forget that whenever they find themselves on a "Patmos," surrounded by an endless raging "sea"—whatever that sea may mean to them—they are not alone. The Patmos experience always results in a revelation of Jesus Christ. It is because Daniel experienced the Babylonian captivity that there is the book of Daniel in the Bible. In the same way, John's Patmos exile produced the book of Revelation. Jesus, who visited John in a vision on that barren island, is the same Jesus who is present with His people to sustain and support them today. He will always be with them, until the very end of the age (see Matthew 28:20).

On the Lord's Day (1:10a)

We do not know how long John was on Patmos before Christ appeared to him in the vision. John briefly states that while he was in the midst of his distress, he was taken into a vision on "the Lord's day" (Revelation 1:10). It appears that, for him, "the Lord's day" was a special day.

In the Bible, there are two days specified as the Lord's. The first one is the seventh-day Sabbath. God calls these seventh-day Sabbaths "My sabbaths" (Exodus 31:13, NASB; Ezekiel 20:12, 20, NASB) and "My holy day" (Isaiah 58:13). Jesus called Himself "Lord of the Sabbath" (Matthew 12:8, NASB; Mark 2:28). This clearly shows that John could have received the vision on the seventh-day Sabbath as the Lord's Day.

Another day referred to as the Lord's in the Bible is the eschatological "day of the Lord," mentioned often in both the Old Testament (Isaiah 13:6–13; Joel 2:11, 31; Amos 5:18–20; Zephaniah 1:14; Malachi 4:5) and the New Testament (1 Thessalonians 5:2; 2 Peter 3:10). It refers to the time when God will bring the history of this world to its end and establish a new order. In the New Testament, the "day of the Lord" refers exclusively to the Second Coming.

It is particularly significant that the Sabbath in the Bible has eschatological significance (Isaiah 58:13, 14; 66:23) and is a sign of deliverance (Deuteronomy 5:15; Ezekiel 20:10–12).

These realities make it reasonable to think that John coined the phrase "the Lord's day" to combine the two biblical concepts into one: to tell his readers that he was taken in vision to the eschatological day of the Lord to witness the events during the conclusion of this earth's history (cf. Revelation 1:7) and to tell them this vision actually took place on the seventh-day Sabbath. This would fit the description of the final events in Revelation and highlight the Sabbath's central role in the end-time drama.

Portrayal of Christ (1:13-16)

Jesus comes to John as the exalted Lord, yet He appears as "one like a son of man" (Revelation 1:13), which is a favorite self-designation of Jesus (Matthew 26:45; Mark 13:26; Luke 19:10). The exalted Christ that John sees in vision has a totally different appearance from the Jesus he knew while in the flesh. The apostle finds human language inadequate to describe Jesus' appearance and resorts to ancient images and Old Testament descriptions of God.

John's portrait of Jesus is similar to the manlike divine figure in Daniel 10:5–12. But Jesus is much more than that. He also bears the characteristics of God in the Old Testament. The phrase "one like a son of man" echoes Daniel 7:13, 14. Jesus has the white hair of "the Ancient of Days" in Daniel 7:9 (NASB). His eyes are like flaming fire; His feet are like burnished bronze; and His face is shining like the divine figure from Daniel's vision (Daniel 10:6; cf. Matthew 17:2). His voice, "like the sound of many waters," was the voice of God in Ezekiel 43:2 (NASB; cf. Daniel 10:6). In the images of this manlike figure, John quickly recognized the glorified Lord with all His divine characteristics and prerogatives.

In applying these Old Testament images to Christ, John uses the words *like* or *as*, which suggest a metaphoric rather than literal meaning. In the ancient world, white or gray hair signified wisdom and experience (Job 15:10; Proverbs 20:29). Christ's eyes, like the flame of fire, indicated His ability to penetrate the innermost secrets of the human heart (Revelation

2:18, 23); His feet, like burnished bronze, symbolized stability and strength (Jeremiah 15:12); His voice, like a trumpet and "the sound of many waters," was the voice of God speaking (Ezekiel 43:2, NASB); and His shining face was referred to in His exaltation (Matthew 17:2, 3). Furthermore, equipped with the two-edged sword coming out of His mouth (Hebrews 4:12), Christ appears and acts as the full authority of God.

In terms of the Old Testament descriptions of God, this portrayal of Jesus appealed to Jews in particular. But for Gentiles, the same description could evoke the image of the Hellenistic goddess Hekate, who was popularly worshiped in western Asia Minor during John's time. Pagans ascribed to her universal authority; they considered her the source and ruler of heaven, earth, and Hades (the underworld), and the agent by which they would come to their end. She manifested herself in three forms, corresponding to each part of the universe: her heavenly form was Selene or Luna (the moon), her earthly form was Artemis or Diana, and her underworld form was Persephone. She was called the "keybearer" because she was thought to possess keys to the gates of Hades. Of her, it was written, "Beginning . . . [and] end . . . are you, and you alone rule all. For all things are from you, and in you do all things. Eternal one, come to their end."[2]

Jesus presents Himself to Gentiles as their only hope. Everything they hoped for in the pagan religion they could find in Christ. His authority surpassed the authority of Hekate and any other authority in heaven, on earth, or under the earth (see Philippians 2:10). By virtue of His own death on the cross, Jesus broke the power of death, and this empowered Him to possess "the keys of Death and Hades" (Revelation 1:18). Because of His death and resurrection, Jesus lives forevermore, being with His people and sustaining them.

The messages to the churches

Jesus provided John with special messages for the churches, and they apply on three levels:

Historical application. It is important to keep in mind that these were actual churches in Asia Minor with real challenges. They were in important, prosperous city centers located on the main postal road that connected them. Under the Roman government, they generally enjoyed peace and prosperity. As a token of their gratitude and loyalty to Rome, a number of cities set up emperor worship in their temples. Emperor worship was compulsory, and the duty of all citizens. The citizens were also expected to be involved in the city's public events and participate in pagan religious ceremonies. Serious consequences awaited those who did not participate, such as the Christians to whom John wrote.

Universal application. Although originally sent *to* the churches in Asia Minor, these messages were not written *only* for them. While Paul wrote his epistles primarily to the churches of his day, they still contain timeless messages for subsequent generations of Christians. Similarly, the messages to the seven churches contain valuable lessons that apply to Christians in all time periods.

These messages were not sent separately but together in one letter (Revelation 1:11). The entire letter was to be read by all the churches. Since each message concludes with an exhortation to heed what the Spirit says to the churches, each message applies to all the churches, although each was written to an individual church. These messages, thus, speak to all Christians and can generally represent different types of Christians in certain periods of history or in different locations.

Prophetic application. Revelation claims to be a book of prophecy and reinforces the prophetic significance of the seven messages (verses 1–3). Furthermore, the spiritual conditions of the seven churches correspond remarkably to the spiritual conditions of Christianity in different periods of history.[3] All this shows that the seven messages are intended to provide, from heaven's perspective, a panoramic survey of Christianity from the first century until the time of the end.

We will examine the struggles of each church, how the message to that church applied then and now, and to which time

26

period the church corresponds. Each message follows the same format, consisting of (1) an address, (2) an introduction of Jesus, (3) Jesus' appraisal of the church, (4) Jesus' counsel and warning to the church, (5) an appeal to hear the Spirit, and (6) promises to the overcomers. By comparing the parallel parts of the messages, we can gain deeper insight into the meaning of these messages.

---

1. See Irenaeus, *Against Heresies* 5.30.3; Eusebius, *Ecclesiastical History* 3.18–20.

2. See David E. Aune, *Revelation 1–5*, Word Biblical Commentary 52a (Dallas, TX: Word Books, 1997), 104–115.

3. See Philip Schaff, *History of the Christian Church*, 3rd ed. (New York: Charles Scribner's Sons, 1910), 1:13–20.

CHAPTER 3

God's People in Cities

Ephesus

At the crossroads of two major trade routes, Ephesus was a famous political, commercial, and religious center. With a population around a quarter of a million people, it was one of the largest cities in the Roman Empire. In the city, there were two temples devoted to the worship of the emperor, along with fifteen temples to other deities. The greatest was the Temple of Artemis (or Diana to the Romans), one of the seven wonders of the ancient world. The city was, however, notorious for crime, immorality, and superstition.

Jesus presents Himself to the church in Ephesus as "the One who holds the seven stars in His right hand, who walks in the midst of the seven golden lampstands" (Revelation 2:1), representing His presence in the church and knowledge of its predicament.

Jesus commends the church for a number of great qualities. In spite of living in a pagan environment, surrounded by pagan lifestyles and immoral practices, the members worked hard and demonstrated patient endurance for the sake of the gospel, standing firm in the face of persecution. The church was also doctrinally sound, exercising discernment in testing false apostles, and not tolerating false teachings (verses 2, 3).

Particularly, they resisted the practices of the Nicolaitans (verse 6). While the precise identity of the Nicolaitans is unclear, some early Christian authors describe them as heretical followers of Nicolas of Antioch, one of the seven deacons of the Jerusalem church, who ultimately fell into heresy (Acts 6:5).[1] The Nicolaitans advocated compromise and conformity with pagan practices to avoid the discomfort and hardships of social isolation and impending persecution. They are also mentioned in the message to the church in Pergamum, in which they are linked with another heretical group: the followers of the teaching of Balaam (Revelation 2:14, 15).

But the church in Ephesus was not enticed by the perverse doctrines of the false teachers. It made every effort to preserve the purity of the gospel and prevent falsehood from corrupting the members, something Ignatius, the bishop of Antioch, would praise the Ephesians for not much later.

In spite of these great qualities, this church had a serious flaw: it was backsliding in love. In their early days, the Christians in Ephesus were known for their "faith in the Lord Jesus" and their "love for all the saints" (Ephesians 1:15, NASB). Now that love was fading. In putting all the emphasis on right actions and sound doctrine, the members were declining in their love for Christ, and as a result, their love for each other had faded. Their religion had become legalistic and loveless. They were doing what was right, but their works were cold and loveless.

The situation of the church in Ephesus reflects the situation of Israel before the Exile, which lost the ardent love and devotion it had for God during their early history (Jeremiah 2:2). Later the Israelites renounced their love for God and abused their fellow humans. As a result, God took from them the privilege of being His light-bearing people. A similar punishment could befall the church in Ephesus. If it does not reflect the love of God, it loses the very reason for its existence and is in danger of having its lampstand removed from its place (Revelation 2:5), which is similar to ancient Israel's loss of this privilege.

Jesus appeals to the church with three imperatives (verse 5). First, the Ephesians must keep remembering. As the Greek text indicates, they had not forgotten the relationship they once had with Christ but had failed to continue in it. By recalling the ardent love for Christ and each other, the members would realize their present spiritual condition.

Then the Ephesians should repent. Repentance in the Bible is closely related to a radical turnaround in one's life. Jesus calls the Ephesians to turn away from their present condition and turn back to God.

Finally, the Ephesians must start doing their first works. Jesus does not urge them to love to the detriment of doing right. The revitalization of their first love, which is for Christ, will result in doing right. If the Christians in Ephesus return to their first devotion to Christ, love for their fellow humans will overflow in their midst.

Throughout history, Christians have always found them-selves strained between strict religious practices and expressing Christ's love. The message to the church in Ephesus is a peren-nial warning to all Christians whose primary concern is doing the right thing. They must always keep in mind the central theme of the gospel: the love of God.

The overcomers in Ephesus—the ones who heed Christ's counsel—are given the promise "to eat from the tree of life, which is in the paradise of God" (verse 7). After Adam and Eve sinned, they were forbidden to eat from the tree of life, but the good news is that those in Ephesus who stay faithful and do not participate in pagan practices will be allowed to eat from the tree in the restored Eden (Revelation 22:2).

The situation of the church in Ephesus corresponds to the situation and spiritual condition of the larger church in the first century. This period of time was characterized by love and faithfulness to the gospel; but by the time John wrote the book of Revelation, the church had begun losing its first love, thus departing from the simplicity and purity of the gospel.

Smyrna

Smyrna stood at a major Greco-Asian trading crossroads and was home to the most convenient and safest harbor in Asia.

Naturally, this made Smyrna a political, religious, and cultural center. Boasting a famous stadium, library, and the largest public theater in the province, it earned the title "the glory of Asia."

The city was also a center of emperor worship. As an act of loyalty, all citizens were required to go to the temple once a year to burn incense before the emperor's statue and proclaim: "Caesar is Lord!" Those who complied received a certificate, allowing them to hold a job or do business; those who did not faced persecution or death.[2]

Jesus introduces Himself to the church in Smyrna as "the first and the last, the One who was dead and came to life" (Revelation 2:8). These characteristics of Jesus correspond aptly with their situation. He understands their position because He was also persecuted to the point of death. They are in extreme poverty; many are jobless and ostracized; some suffered imprisonment and even death—all for Christ. Jews who were distancing themselves from Christians and slandered them were referred to by Jesus as the "synagogue of Satan" (verse 9).

The Christians in Smyrna understandably lived in constant fear; unfortunately, as Jesus warned, ten days of persecution lay ahead. But Jesus urged them to remain faithful, even to the point of death, and they would receive "the crown of life" (verse 10). The garland given to the winner at the ancient Olympic Games was hardly everlasting, but the crown Jesus promises the faithful in Smyrna is eternal life, to be given at His second coming (2 Timothy 4:8).

The overcomers in Smyrna are given the promise that they will not be hurt by the second death (see Revelation 2:11). Physical death is a temporary sleep and thus not a tragedy because of the hope of the resurrection. It is the second death that should be feared: eternal death, from which there will be no resurrection.

The experience of the church in Smyrna coincided with the severe persecution of Christians throughout the Roman Empire during the second and third centuries. The "ten days" (verse 10) mentioned in the message could be applied prophetically to the notorious imperial persecution initiated by the emperor

Diocletian and continued under his successor Galerius (A.D. 303–313). In this way, the church in Smyrna could represent the period in church history from the beginning of the second century until approximately A.D. 313, when Constantine the Great issued the famous Edict of Milan, granting Christians religious freedom.

Pergamum

For more than two and a half centuries, Pergamum served as the political, intellectual, and religious capital of Asia and was one of the elite cities of the Hellenistic world. It boasted a library that rivaled Alexandria with nearly two hundred thousand volumes. Of all the magnificent temples to Athena, Dionysus, and Asclepius, the enormous altar to Zeus, with smoke constantly rising from it, was the crown jewel. Stories of miraculous healings by "the Savior" Asclepius, the Greek god of healing, came out of the immense *asclepeion* just outside the city. This saturation of paganism truly made Pergamum the place "where Satan dwells" (verse 13).

Jesus comes as "the One who has the sharp two-edged sword" (verse 12). The Roman governor had *ius gladii* (the right of the sword)—the power of execution,[3] a power frequently wielded against Christians. But the power over life and death belongs only to Jesus (cf. Revelation 1:17, 18).

Jesus knew that the Pergamum Christians lived at the very heart of Satan's activities. They had been ostracized for their refusal to condone emperor worship and honor the pagan gods. Some, such as Antipas, had paid with their lives. Yet most had remained unwaveringly faithful in the face of this persecution.

Jesus goes on to single out those who were compromising their Christianity: the Nicolaitans and those "who hold to the teaching of Balaam" (Revelation 2:14, 15). Like Balaam who seduced the Israelites to engage in illicit relationships with Moabite women and practice idolatry (Numbers 31:16), these people encouraged their fellow Christians to compromise on emperor worship and other pagan socioreligious activities

(Revelation 2:14), as opposed to the church in Ephesus, which strongly resisted the Nicolaitans.

Jesus encourages them to resist compromise with paganism and warns that if they do not repent, He will come against them with the two-edged sword of judgment in His mouth (verses 12, 16). As Balaam was killed with the sword (Joshua 13:22), so will the Nicolaitans be judged. The only way to avoid this doom is to repent and make a decisive turnaround in their relationship with Christ.

In addition to hidden manna, which is "the bread of angels" (Psalm 78:25, NASB), Christ promises the overcomers that He will replace the Roman-issued business certificates, which they were denied because of the refusal to participate in emperor worship, with white stones engraved with new names. These stones will grant them privileges far beyond any pagan pleasure.

After the church finally won its struggle with paganism in A.D. 313 following Constantine the Great's conversion, Christians no longer feared persecution or external pressure. Nevertheless, compromise still plagued the church as pagan philosophies and customs crept in, gradually replacing the Bible as the source of teaching and belief. While many remained unwaveringly faithful, the fourth and fifth centuries witnessed spiritual decline and apostasy as the church wrestled with the temptation of compromise.

Thyatira

Thyatira, home to local trade guilds instead of regional temples or administrative centers, was the least substantial of the seven cities addressed in Revelation. These guilds controlled the numerous trades in the city, and one could not conduct business without membership. Each guild, however, had a patron god with accompanying festivals, often with immoral activities such as using temple prostitutes. Refusal to participate resulted in dire consequences, severe sanctions, or expulsion from the guilds. These penalties were a significant challenge for Christians living in the first century.

To Thyatira, Jesus comes as the Son of God. His flaming eyes signify His ability to see what is in the innermost parts of humans (Revelation 2:23)—searching minds and hearts (the seat of intelligence)—an ability belonging only to God (Jeremiah 17:10). Christ's burnished bronze feet emphasize His uncompromising stance against seductive influences in the church.

Jesus describes the Thyatira church as loving, faithful, service oriented, and perseverant. In contrast to Ephesus, their latter works of love are greater than the first. In the New Testament, love and faith go together (Galatians 5:6; Ephesians 1:15; 1 Thessalonians 3:6); furthermore, service is an outcome of love, and perseverance is a product of faith (Colossians 1:23; 2 Thessalonians 1:3, 4).

Yet Thyatira has tolerated an influential woman, who Jesus nicknames Jezebel. In the Old Testament, Jezebel was Ahab's notorious queen who led Israel into apostasy (1 Kings 16:31–33). Similar to the Nicolaitans, this "Jezebel" claimed to be God's prophetess, stating that it was all right for Christians to go along with guild requirements (Revelation 2:20), and "things sacrificed to idols and to commit fornication" (verses 14, 15). Her influence led many to compromise with paganism.

Jezebel's spiritual harlotry foreruns the great Babylon harlot, who at the time of the end will seduce the world's leaders into the service of Satan (Revelation 17:1–7). Since the harlot's activities take place in bed, the bed is where Jezebel and her consorts—those who condone her teachings—will be judged. Jesus will throw them and their offspring into tremendous affliction if they do not repent, stressing the seriousness of their actions.

To the remnant who have not experimented with Jezebel's arcane knowledge, Jesus promises not to add to their burdens, simply exhorting them to hold fast to what they have. Furthermore, He promises the faithful a share in His victory, granting them authority over the nations (Revelation 2:26, 27). He also gives them the morning star, which is a symbol of Jesus (Revelation 22:16). All of this means that Jesus ultimately gives them Himself, the greatest gift of all.

35

During the Middle Ages, the church faced dangers not from without but within. Those who claimed divine authority placed tradition above the Bible. A human priesthood and sacred relics replaced Christ's priesthood, and works became the means of salvation. Those who defended a biblical faith faced severe persecution and death.

Sardis

Sardis had a splendid history. Six centuries earlier, it had been one of the greatest cities in the world as the capital of the opulent Lydian kingdom. It was known as a trading center for wool, dyeing, and garment-making industries, providing its citizens with a luxurious lifestyle. Located on a particularly steep hill with only one access route, the city was a natural fortress. Understandably, the citizens were overconfident, carelessly guarding the city walls, if at all. Yet the city was captured by surprise on two occasions, first by Cyrus the Great of Persia (547 B.C.) and later by Antiochus III (214/13 B.C.). On both occasions, enemy soldiers climbed the precipice by night and found the walls unguarded, quickly storming the arrogant and defenseless city.

Jesus' tone is alarming and sharp from the start, giving only rebuke. It is not for any specific sin but for spiritual complacency and lethargy. Despite the church's reputation for being alive, He finds it spiritually dead, reflecting a city existing on a past reputation. Sardis's works do not measure up, lacking the transforming power of the gospel (Revelation 3:2). Its compromises with the pagan environment had effectively killed its spirituality and witness.

Jesus encourages the church to keep watch and to remember how they heard and received the gospel at the beginning (verses 2, 3). The only way to rekindle their devotion to God is to keep past experiences fresh in their minds and apply them to the present. The resulting repentance will snap them out of their lethargy and, by the Spirit of God, reenergize their love and devotion.

But if they do not repent, Jesus will unexpectedly come

against them in judgment, like a thief in the night. If the church fails to watch, its destiny will mirror the city's history; twice being unexpectedly conquered due to a lack of vigilance. Similarly, Christ will visit them in judgment, and if they fail to keep watch, it will be too late to repent (verse 3b).

Yet not all have spiritually died. Some have kept their clothes clean of paganism (verses 2, 4). Jesus promises they are worthy of walking with Him in white robes, which symbolizes their faithfulness to Him; the fulfilment of the promise is described in Revelation 7:9–17. To those who overcome, Jesus will give white robes and a promise not to erase their names from the book of life, confessing their names before the Father and His angels.

This period of church history saw Protestant Scholasticism, following the rejuvenation brought by the Reformation, plunge the church into lifeless formalism. Progressively, people focused on doctrinal polemics and controversies, degenerating into a state of spiritual lethargy. By the end, the rising tide of philosophical rationalism and secularism overwhelmed the saving grace of the gospel, giving place to rationalism and theological arguments. Despite the appearance of vitality, the church was actually dead.

Philadelphia

Philadelphia was a prosperous city that stood on the imperial trade road, connecting all parts east with all parts west. From its inception, Philadelphia was intended to serve as a missionary city for promoting the Greek language and culture in the areas of Lydia and Phrygia. Its geographical location, however, made it subject to occasional earthquakes. The most severe one took place in A.D. 17, devastating Philadelphia, Sardis, and other surrounding cities.

Jesus' presentation to Philadelphia is rich with Old Testament allusions. "The Holy One" is a description of God (Revelation 3:7; cf. Isaiah 43:15; 54:5; Habakkuk 3:3), as well as a New Testament designation for Jesus (Mark 1:24; John 6:69). His possession of David's key is an allusion to Isaiah 22:22.

Jesus is the One with full authority and access to the heavenly storehouse, explaining why He is able to make great promises to His church.

In contrast to Sardis, Philadelphia does not receive any rebuke. They have kept Jesus' word and have not denied Him (Revelation 3:8b). Like the Smyrnaeans, they also suffer from Jewish opposition, but Jesus assures the church He is already dealing with their opponents. The day is coming when those who harm them will be forced to admit that God is with them.

But this church is not spiritually strong. Like Sardis, they suffer from the influence of their pagan environment, which significantly impacts their spiritual life and witness. Despite their weakness, Christ promises to set before them an open door of opportunities. When He opens that door, not even all the power of the enemy will be able to shut it.

Jesus also promises to preserve the Philadelphians during the time of severe trial that is to befall the wicked, coming on "those who dwell on the earth" (Revelation 3:10). Despite the hard times approaching, Jesus promises to protect His faithful people during this time of trial. All He asks is that they hang on with what little spark of faithfulness they have. If they do, neither Satan nor humans will be able to take the crown of victory reserved for them.

The overcomers are promised to be permanent pillars— symbols of the New Testament church (1 Timothy 3:15)—in the temple in the New Jerusalem, with the names of God, the New Jerusalem, and Christ written on them. The faithful are promised that they will always be in God's presence and serve Him in His temple (Revelation 7:15).

The situation of the church in Philadelphia compares with the situation in Christianity during the eighteenth and nineteenth centuries, which is a period characterized by a great revival in Protestantism. Various movements revitalized genuine faith in the saving grace of Christ, resulting in a restoration of the spirit of Christian fellowship and self-sacrifice. The church during this period was driven by a genuine desire to carry the gospel to the whole world. During this time, there was a more sizable circulation of the gospel than ever before.

Laodicea

Because of its favorable location on the major trade road between Ephesus and Syria, Laodicea was one of the great commercial centers of the ancient world. Its wealth came largely from the luxurious black wool used for clothing manufacturing and its position as a great banking center, storing large quantities of gold.

Laodicea also boasted a medical school that produced an eye ointment made from Phrygian powder mixed with oil. The city was so wealthy it rejected imperial assistance after a devastating earthquake in A.D. 60, commenting that help was unnecessary. Indeed, the only drawback was the lack of water, which was brought to the city by a six-mile aqueduct. Fed by both a hot spring and cool mountain water, the city gained a reputation of having lukewarm water.

Laodicea is in such bad shape that Jesus has nothing positive to say. Despite the absence of specific charges of sin, apostasy, or heresy, no other church receives such a stern rebuke from Jesus. He likens the city's water supply to the members, neither refreshingly cold nor hot but lukewarm, and as such, He is about to vomit them out of His mouth (Revelation 3:16).

The church reflects the complacency of a self-assured city. Believing their wealth is a sign of divine favor, they feel no need. Sadly, their material wealth does not translate to spiritual wealth. If anything, they experience the exact opposite effect. In this case, the Greek word for "poor" (*ptóchos*) means *extreme poverty*. In addition, their lack of spiritual self-awareness has left them spiritually blind. How ironic for a city known for its eye treatments!

Jesus counsels the church to buy from Him three things. The first is gold refined in fire that would make the Laodiceans truly rich—a symbol of tested, proven faith (1 Peter 1:7). Second, Jesus offers white garments to cover their nakedness—a symbol of salvation (Revelation 3:4–6; 7:9, 13, 14; Isaiah 61:10) and a right relationship with God (Revelation 3:4).

Finally, He offers eye salve to heal their eyes, so they may accurately see their condition and the value of the inheritance Christ makes available to them (cf. Ephesians 1:17, 18). That these items are not available for free indicates that the Laodiceans must give something in exchange for what they need. What they must surrender is their pride, complacency, and self-sufficiency in order to receive the riches of Christ.

Jesus has not given up on them and is doing everything possible to make them realize their condition and break the chains of self-sufficiency. The only remedy is true repentance and a fresh start with Christ. Jesus concludes His appeal with the striking image of Him standing at the door and knocking (Revelation 3:20; cf. Song of Solomon 5:2–6). Suddenly, Jesus is addressing individuals within the church. Those who open the door to Him will enjoy an intimate, loving dinner with Christ, indicating a deep and personal relationship.

Typically, the number of promises is in proportion to the decline of the church's spiritual condition. But Laodicea receives only one promise: to share Jesus' throne. But this promise, fulfilled when Christ returns to earth (Revelation 20:4–6), encompasses every other promise given. To sit with Jesus on His throne is to have everything.

The self-sufficiency and lukewarm attitude of Laodicea echoes our own condition. We struggle with authenticity and doing more than simply going through the motions. The times are urgent, and we face political, religious, and secular upheaval not experienced by previous generations. Christ's warning to Laodicea is a direct message to us and has far-reaching implications for all who live at the close of earth's history.

---

1. Irenaeus, *Against Heresies* 1.26.3; 3.11, in *The Ante-Nicene Fathers*, vol. 1, ed. A. Roberts and J. Donaldson (New York: Charles Scribner's Sons, 1913), 352, 426–429; Hippolytus of Rome, *The Refutation of All Heresies* 7.24, in *The Ante-Nicene Fathers*, vol. 5, ed. A. Roberts and J. Donaldson (New York: Charles Scribner's Sons, 1919),115.

2. See William Barclay, *The Revelation of John*, The Daily Study Bible, 2nd ed. (Philadelphia, PA: Westminster John Knox Press, 1976), 1:76–78.

3. William Ramsay, *The Letters to the Seven Churches*, 2nd ed. (Peabody, MA: Hendrickson, 1994), 214.

The Enthronement of the Lamb

The scene in Revelation 4 and 5 is introductory and does not fit into the chronological sequence of the vision. Before the future is revealed to John, he is taken into the heavenly throne room and given a glimpse of Christ's exaltation on the throne at the right hand of the Father, giving heaven's perspective on what future events mean. As history unfolds, Jesus Christ, the Sovereign Ruler of the universe, will bring the events of this world to their conclusion and deal decisively with the problem of sin.

The throne room (4:2, 3, 5, 6)

When it comes to God, John does not attempt to describe Him using the anthropomorphic language used by the Old Testament prophets. Instead, he focuses on God's radiant glory. The Old Testament often speaks of the splendid glory surrounding God (Psalm 104:1, 2; Ezekiel 1:26–28), which can hardly be expressed in human language.

John describes it in terms of dazzling precious stones: jasper, sardius (carnelian), and emerald (Revelation 4:3). Adding to the splendor of the scene is the flashing brilliance of a rainbow surrounding the throne (verse 3b). Centuries earlier, Ezekiel witnessed in vision a rainbow around God's throne, signifying "the likeness of the glory of the LORD" (Ezekiel 1:28, NASB). And long before Ezekiel, God gave the rainbow to Noah as a sign of His covenant with humankind. The rainbow John observes, radiating from the precious stones, is intended to provide confidence in God's covenant promise to His people and in His faithfulness to that promise (Genesis 9:12–17).

Before the throne, there is a flat expanse that appeared to John like "a sea of glass, like crystal" (Revelation 4:6), echoing Ezekiel's vision (Ezekiel 1:22). Centuries earlier, God was seen by Moses and the elders as standing on something that "appeared to be a pavement of sapphire, as clear as the sky itself" (Exodus 24:10, NASB).

Finally, John observes flashes of lightning, sounds, and peals of thunder issuing from the throne (Revelation 4:5). They accentuate the splendor and evoke the giving of the law to Moses at Mount Sinai (Exodus 19:16; 20:18), when Israel, having been redeemed from Egypt, was inaugurated as the people of God and as "a kingdom of priests" (Exodus 19:6, NASB). In similar fashion, John now observes as Christ, having redeemed humanity by His blood, receives the sealed scroll from God and inaugurates the redeemed as "a kingdom and priests" to God (Revelation 5:10).[1]

The throne-room assembly (4:4-11)

The throne room of the heavenly temple is a grand, majestic place, accommodating countless heavenly beings. John specifies four distinct groups of participants in the scene.

The Members of the Godhead. The first person John observes in the throne room is God the Father sitting on the throne (Revelation 4:2). He is the object of worship for the entire heavenly assembly. Next is the Holy Spirit, the Second Member of the Godhead (cf. Revelation 1:4). He is referred to as "the seven Spirits of God" and is symbolized by the seven torches of fire before the throne (Revelation 4:5). The phrase "the seven Spirits of God" denotes the fullness and universality of the work of the Holy Spirit in the church. Apparently absent is the Third Member of the Godhead. Jesus does not appear in the scene until chapter 5, when He is greeted and worshiped by the whole heavenly assembly.

The twenty-four elders (4:4). In a circle around the throne, there are twenty-four other thrones, with twenty-four elders sitting on them. They are dressed in white and wear gold crowns. Who are these elders? Some view them as a group of angels. But nowhere in the Bible or Jewish tradition are angels ever called elders, and the elders and the angels are clearly distinguished in Revelation 7:11. Furthermore, the elders share God's throne, while angels always stand in God's presence. The elders represent the overcomers, who receive the promise to sit with Jesus Christ on His throne (Revelation 3:21). They also wear white robes, which is the attire of God's faithful people (Revelation 3:4, 5, 18; 6:11; 7:9, 13, 14). Finally, they have golden victory crowns on their heads, reserved exclusively for the triumphant saints (Revelation 2:10; 3:11; cf. 2 Timothy 4:8; James 1:12). These victory crowns are not royal crowns. Rather, they show that the twenty-four elders are victorious humans, not rulers from the other worlds.

All these details point to the twenty-four elders being a symbolic group, representative of redeemed humanity. The two sets of twelve refer to the twelve tribes of Israel as the symbol of God's people in the Old Testament and the twelve apostles as the symbol of God's people in the New Testament. In the New Jerusalem, the twelve gates are named after the twelve tribes of Israel, and the twelve foundations are named after the twelve apostles (Revelation 21:12–14). The twenty-four elders, thus, represent the entire body of God's people from both the Old and New Testaments—the church in its totality.

In the Old Testament temple, there were twenty-four divisions of priests who took turns in the temple services (1 Chronicles 24:4–19). Each division was led by a chief priest, with twenty-four chief priests in total (verse 5). In Jewish tradition, these chief priests were called "elders." Similarly, the singers in the temple were organized into twenty-four groups (1 Chronicles 25:8–31). Notice that the activities of the twenty-four elders in Revelation consist of continuous worship and adoration to God (Revelation 5:9, 10; 19:4) and the presentation of the saints' prayers to God mirrors the work of the priests and singers in the earthly temple. Therefore, seated on the thrones, the twenty-four elders function in their twofold role as priests and kings (cf. Revelation 5:8–10).

The four living beings (4:6b–8). On each side of the throne there are four heavenly beings facing the four cardinal directions. They are unlike any heavenly being John had seen before and are quite similar to the cherubim in Ezekiel's vision of God's throne (Ezekiel 1:5–14; 10:12–15). Both Ezekiel and John saw the same number of beings and both refer to them as "four living beings." Both compare their appearance to a lion, a calf or an ox, a man, and a flying eagle; and in both cases, they are covered with eyes. Finally, both visions closely associate them with the throne.

While the living beings in Ezekiel's vision have four faces and four wings (Ezekiel 1:6), the four living beings in Revelation have six wings like the seraphim in Isaiah's vision (Isaiah 6:2). Like the seraphim in Isaiah's vision, the four living beings in Revelation 4 unceasingly praise God with these words of acclamation: "Holy, holy, holy Lord God, the Almighty" (Revelation 4:8; cf. Isaiah 6:3).

All this indicates that the four living beings are exalted angels close to God, who serve Him as agents and guardians of His throne. They are always seen in proximity to the throne (Revelation 4:6; 5:6; 14:3), and their association with the throne is reminiscent of the cherubim on the ark of the covenant. These cherubim faced each other with their wings stretched over the mercy seat (Exodus 25:18–21; 1 Kings 6:23–28), where God is described as sitting (2 Kings 19:15; Psalms 80:1; 99:1; Isaiah 37:16).

The portrayal of the living beings is symbolic. Their wings point to their swiftness in carrying out God's orders, and the eyes represent their intelligence and discernment. Their appearances in terms of a lion, a calf or an ox, a man, and a flying eagle represent the entire order of creation. As representatives of the entire creation, they are constantly engaged in leading the heavenly hosts in worship and praise to God (Revelation 4:8, 9; 5:8, 9, 14; 7:11, 12; 19:4), as well as being the divine agents involved in the execution of God's wrath upon the earth (Revelation 6:1, 3, 5, 7; 15:7).

The heavenly hosts. The largest group in the throne room assembly consists of the multitude of the angelic hosts; the number of which is "myriads of myriads and thousands of thousands" (Revelation 5:11). Ellen G. White suggests that, since this group is joined in their praises by "every creature" (verse 13), they are envoys from the rest of the universe, representing the unfallen worlds.[2] These envoys, together with the twenty-four elders and the four living beings, are assembled in the heavenly throne room to celebrate Christ's triumph over Satan and to express their approval and endorsement of His enthronement.

The seven-sealed scroll (5:1)

The magnificent liturgy in the throne room is interrupted for a moment as everyone's eyes focus on the throne. The Greek text clearly shows that the scroll John saw was on the throne at the right hand of God. To sit at the right side of the king was the highest place of honor (cf. 1 Kings 2:19), and the Israelites understood that the king in Israel sat at God's right side as coruler with Him (Psalms 80:17; 110:1). The scroll lying on the throne implies that the person who takes the scroll is to take its place on the throne. Thus, when Jesus, a few moments later, picks up the scroll (Revelation 5:8), He takes His seat on the throne at the right hand of the Father, thereby assuming His role as the new ruler of the Davidic royal line (verse 5).

The scroll is "sealed with seven seals" (verse 1). In ancient times, ratification of a legal document was accomplished with an impression made by a ring at the end of the content. To prevent tampering, it was also rolled up and tied with threads. The seal was impressed in blobs of clay or wax where the threads knotted. The document could not be opened nor its contents disclosed without breaking the seal. Only an authorized person could break the seals and open the document without consequence.

In John's day, the practice of sealing documents with more than one seal was common. Roman law dictated that some documents had to be sealed with a minimum of seven seals. The symbolic scroll John saw in vision was like a legal document rolled up, tied with a cord, and sealed along the outside edge with seals of wax affixed to the knots. As such, it could not be opened nor could its contents be disclosed until all seven seals were broken.[3]

Daniel and Revelation show that if a message is to be understood at a later time, sealing is God's way of concealing the revelation until the appointed time (Daniel 12:4, 9; Revelation 10:4). The scroll in Revelation 5 is sealed for the obvious purpose of concealing its contents and keeping them hidden. Because it is sealed, nobody is "able to open the scroll or to look into it" (Revelation 5:3). It is not possible to open it unless an authorized person breaks all the seals.

Revelation 10:7 shows that its contents are related to "the mystery of God" (NASB) and His purpose in resolving sin, saving fallen humanity, and establishing His eternal kingdom. This mystery has been hidden for ages, but it has been partially revealed with the coming of Christ and the preaching of the gospel (Romans 16:25, 26; Ephesians 3:1–12). Ellen G. White comments that the sealed scroll contains the record of the great controversy, which includes, "the roll of the history of God's providences, the prophetic history of nations and the church. Herein was contained the divine utterances, His authority, His commandments, His laws, the whole symbolic counsel of the Eternal, and the history of all ruling powers in the nations. In symbolic language was contained in that roll the influence of every nation, tongue, and people from the beginning of earth's history to its close."[4]

The sealed scroll, thus, functions as a symbolic reference to the divine plan of salvation. If the scroll is sealed, the plan of salvation remains unrealized. When the final seal is broken at the sound of the seventh trumpet—the Second Coming—then the plan of salvation will be ultimately realized (Revelation 10:7).

The enthronement of Christ (5:7-14)

Revelation 5 describes the enthronement of Jesus in the heavenly temple after His ascension into heaven. The language used to portray the scene is connected with the Israelite kings in the Old Testament. The seven-sealed scroll John saw Jesus take from the throne at the right hand of the Father is comparable to the covenant scroll of the law that was handed to the Israelite kings at their enthronement. To take the scroll symbolized the right to sit on the throne and reign. To unfold the scroll meant to unfold God's plan of salvation for fallen humanity.

Christ's victory on the cross made Him worthy to take and unseal the covenant scroll, which, because of human disobedience, was sealed. In the heavenly throne room, when Christ the Lamb approached the throne to take the scroll, an anthem of praise and adoration arose from the heavenly assembly, acknowledging that act (Revelation 5:7–14). This was the climactic moment of the scene. The covenant book, which had been sealed and stored for ages, was handed to the triumphant Christ—the long-awaited King of the Davidic lineage and the Lion from the tribe of Judah.

Since the scroll signifies the right to reign, the symbolic act of taking the scroll makes Christ the rightful King over the universe. He takes His seat on the throne and shares the ruling prerogatives with the Father (Revelation 3:21). The Father now governs the universe through the Son. All authority and sovereignty are given to Him (see Matthew 28:18). Christ is now "far above all rule and authority and power and dominion, and every name that is named, not only in this age but also in the one to come" (Ephesians 1:21, NASB).

The symbolic taking of the scroll by Christ the Lamb signified the transference of authority from Satan to Christ. As the scholar Adela Yarbro Collins notes, "The problem facing the heavenly council is the rebellion of Satan which is paralleled by rebellion on earth."[5] Dismayed by these circumstances, the tears of John "express the desire of the faithful to have this situation rectified."[6] With the fall of the human race into the bondage of sin, humanity became lost and hopeless. By

47

usurping lordship and dominion of earth (cf. Luke 4:6), Satan became "the ruler of this world" (John 12:31, NASB; cf. John 14:30; 16:11).

But what was lost with Adam has now been regained by Christ. His installment on the heavenly throne demonstrates that His sacrifice has been accepted on behalf of humanity. The death of Jesus purchased people for God from every tribe, language, people, and nation (Revelation 5:9).

In Revelation 5, Christ has been inaugurated into His royal and priestly ministry in the heavenly sanctuary. By receiving the scroll, He takes the destiny of all humanity into His hands. His ability to break the seals and open the scroll entitles Him to carry the plan of salvation to its ultimate realization. The scroll contains the terms and conditions of God's promise to His people. It points to their only hope, that their Lord reigns on the throne of the universe. He will be forever with them, to sustain and protect them until He returns to take them home.

The Pentecost scene

The installment of Christ on the heavenly throne took place at the time of Pentecost (Acts 2:32–36).[7] During His installment at the right hand of the Father, Jesus became the legitimate Ruler of earth. The Holy Spirit descended on the disciples to fulfill the promise Jesus made to them (John 14:16–18). Revelation 5:6 mentions the seven Spirits "sent into all the earth." The seven Spirits denote the fullness of the Holy Spirit's activity in the world (seven is a number of fullness). While earlier in the book the Holy Spirit is regularly before the throne (cf. Revelation 1:4; 4:5), in chapter 5 He is sent to the earth. Sending the Holy Spirit is directly related to the inauguration of Christ's post-Calvary ministry.

The Holy Spirit's work on earth in connection with Christ's exaltation to the heavenly throne is significant. According to John 7:39, the Holy Spirit "was not yet given, because Jesus was not yet glorified" (NASB). But in his Pentecost sermon, Peter explained that the coming of the Holy Spirit to earth was the result of Christ's exaltation on the heavenly throne at the right hand of God (Acts 2:32–36). The coming of the Holy Spirit at Pentecost was heaven's assurance that Jesus had appeared before the Father and that His sacrifice had been accepted on behalf of humanity. After this, Jesus was inaugurated into His post-Calvary ministry as our King and Priest. He is now our Mediator in the heavenly sanctuary, and through Him, fallen humans have access to God.

Christ is now exalted on the throne of the universe and inaugurated into His post-Calvary ministry, and the work of the Holy Spirit continues to apply His victorious death to the lives of humans and announces God's kingdom throughout the earth. Pentecost marks the beginning of spreading the gospel throughout the world, and its continued proclamation is expanding the kingdom by winning human hearts. For those who respond to the gospel, divine grace is available. For those who reject the gospel, consequences are inevitable. This sets the stage for the scene in Revelation 6—the opening of the seven seals.

1. Richard M. Davidson, "Sanctuary Typology," in *Symposium on Revelation—Book 1*, ed. Frank B. Holbrook, Daniel and Revelation Committee Series 6 (Silver Spring, MD: Biblical Research Institute, 1992), 123.

2. Ellen G. White, *The Desire of Ages* (Nampa, ID: Pacific Press®, 1989), 834.

3. George Eldon Ladd, *A Commentary on the Revelation of John* (Grand Rapids, MI: Eerdmans, 1972), 81.

4. Ellen G. White, "MR No. 667—Prophetic Interpretation," in *Manuscript Releases*, vol. 9 (Silver Spring, MD: Ellen G. White Estate, 1990), 7.

5. Adela Yarbro Collins, *The Apocalypse*, New Testament Message 22 (Collegeville, MN: Liturgical Press, 1979), 39.

6. Yarbro Collins, *The Apocalypse*, 39.

7. The New Testament is replete with texts stating that at His ascension, Christ was seated at the right side of God and has been given authority, power, and universal dominion (Romans 8:34; Ephesians 1:20–22; Colossians 3:1; Hebrews 10:12; 12:2; 1 Peter 3:21, 22).

The Seven Seals

The seven seals of Revelation review the same history as the seven churches. Beginning with the famous four horsemen of the Apocalypse, the seals describe the experience of the church through the ages. The key to unlocking the theological meaning of the four horsemen and the rest of the seals lies in the Old Testament covenant relationship between God and Israel. In the New Testament, the key that helps explain the seals is a proper understanding of Jesus' apocalyptic sermon on the Mount of Olives.

In the Old Testament, God made a covenant with Israel at Sinai, promising that if the people obeyed Him, He would recognize them as His chosen people (Exodus 19:5, 6). As long as the Israelites stayed within the covenant relationship, God vowed to bless them. The books of Leviticus and Deuteronomy (particularly Leviticus 26:3–9 and Deuteronomy 28) contain a long list of blessings for the Israelites if they lived according to God's instruction. Conversely, if the Israelites broke the covenant, a series of curses would ensue (Leviticus 26:21–36; Deuteronomy 32:23–25). These warnings include four plagues—wild beasts, the sword, pestilence, and famine—that would come upon Israel for breaking the covenant. In order to win the people back, the curses functioned as disciplinary measures by which God chastised His people when they wandered away. He promised to forgive His people if they repented and turned back to Him.

Revelation graphically describes the experience of the church from Pentecost to the Second Coming through covenant curse imagery. The four horsemen symbolize the overcoming experience of God's people, entitling them to share Jesus' throne (cf. Revelation 3:21). The white horse rider symbolizes the victorious spread of the gospel. But as it is preached, Christians fall into unfaithfulness and disobedience. Therefore, God allows the world to chastise them like Israel of old. The rider on the fiery-red horse brings persecution; the rider on the black horse brings spiritual famine; and the rider on the ashen-gray horse brings spiritual plague and death. The graphic picture of the four horsemen delivers a solemn warning to Christians throughout history: do not take Christ's gospel lightly.

There is also a close correlation between the seven seals and the Synoptic Apocalypse (Matthew 24; Mark 13; Luke 21), which is a discourse Jesus delivered shortly before His crucifixion. In this speech, Jesus explained what would happen up to the end time.

Jesus first described the general realities of the Christian era in terms of wars and rumors of wars, famine, pestilence, persecution, earthquakes, deception, and heavenly signs (Matthew 24:4–14); these events also occur in Revelation 6. Second, Jesus talked about a long interval in history from the destruction of Jerusalem until the great tribulation, during which God's people would experience heightened persecution (verses 15–28). Third, Jesus pointed to the heavenly signs that indicate the nearness of the Second Coming, followed by specific signs announcing the coming of Christ in power and glory (verses 29–31).

These comparisons show that both Matthew 24:4–14 and the first four seals (Revelation 6:1–8) refer to the general realities of the Christian age. The horsemen and the covenant curses in Leviticus 26 have the same function as the general signs foretold by Jesus (Matthew 24:4–14). These signs keep God's people awake and remind them of the reality of Christ's return.

The first seal (6:1, 2)

As Christ the Lamb opens the first seal, a white horse steps onto the scene. The rider on the horse holds a bow and is given a crown. The Greek word used for "crown" is *stephanos*, "the crown of victory" (cf. 2 Timothy 4:8), which was a garland given to winners at the ancient Olympic Games. This rider is a conqueror, going forth to completely conquer. In John's day, Roman generals would ride white horses to celebrate a great victory.

This scene is symbolic. In the Old Testament, God is sometimes pictured as riding a horse with a bow in His hand, conquering the enemies of His people (Psalm 45:4, 5; Habakkuk 3:8–13). Revelation 19:11–16 portrays Christ as riding a white horse, leading the heavenly armies into the final battle of this earth's history. Furthermore, in Revelation white is a symbol of purity and is regularly associated with Christ and His followers. Also, the *stephanos* crown worn by the horseman is often associated with Christ and His victorious people. Finally, the concept of conquering clearly echoes the Revelation 3:21 and 5:5 references to Christ's overcoming on Calvary.

The rider on the white horse signifies the spread of the gospel of Jesus Christ, starting with Pentecost. Just prior to this event, Christ was exalted to the right hand of the Father on the heavenly throne, beginning the expansion of His kingdom by waging warfare against the forces of evil. There were many territories to conquer and many people to win for the kingdom. In its initial stage, the proclamation of the gospel had a powerful start as a result of the manifestation of the Holy Spirit's power. Thousands were converted in one day (Acts 2:41, 47; 4:4), and this "conquest of the gospel" will continue throughout history until the ultimate triumph is realized at the time of the end (cf. Matthew 24:14).

The second seal (6:3, 4)

Christ's opening of the second seal ushers a fiery-red horse onto the scene. Red is the color of blood and corresponds to the mission of this horse. The rider, who has a large sword, does not do the killing himself. Instead, he takes away peace from the earth, and people slay one another.

The first horseman shows that through preaching the gospel, Christ is waging spiritual warfare against the forces of evil. But the forces of evil render strong resistance to the gospel, rallying those who reject it against those who accept it. Inevitably, persecution follows.

Of course, the record shows that the gospel always divides people. While its acceptance brings peace, its rejection results in a loss of peace. "Do not think that I came to bring peace on the earth," Jesus said. "I did not come to bring peace, but a sword. For I came to set a man against his father, and a daughter against her mother, and a daughter-in-law against her mother-in-law; and a man's enemies will be the members of his household" (Matthew 10:34–36, NASB). As in the Old Testament, the enemies of God's people often turned against each other, so in the second seal scene, those who resist and reject the gospel turn against each other in persecution.

The third seal (6:5-6)

The third seal reveals a black horse. Its rider is seen holding a scale for weighing food. John also hears an announcement by one of the four living beings: "A quart of wheat for a denarius, and three quarts of barley for a denarius, and do not harm the oil and the wine" (Revelation 6:6).

In Palestine, grain, oil, and wine were the three main crops. They are mentioned in the Old Testament as the basic necessities of life. As part of the covenant blessings, God promises Israel it would have food in abundance; but the careful measuring described in the third seal indicates great scarcity or famine, which is part of the covenant curses (cf. Leviticus 26:26; Ezekiel 4:16). In John's day, a denarius was a daily wage (cf. Matthew 20:2); and in normal circumstances, it would buy the necessities for a family. But in famine conditions the price would be greatly inflated. In the third seal scene, it would take a day's wage to buy enough food for just one person, since a quart of wheat was the daily ration for one person. To feed a small family, a day's wage would buy three quarts of barley—a cheaper, coarser food for the poor.

The imagery of the black horse and its rider points to what will befall those who reject the gospel. Corresponding to the mission of the horse and its rider, black is the opposite of white and denotes the absence of the gospel. In Scripture, grain symbolizes the Word of God (Luke 8:11), and bread also stands for the words of Jesus (John 6:35–58). The rejection of the gospel results in a famine of God's Word that is similar to the spiritual famine prophesied by Amos concerning the Israelites (Amos 8:11–13).

But the famine of the third seal is not fatal. The same voice that commissioned the horseman also announces that the oil and wine will not be affected by the famine but will continue to be available. Spiritually, oil symbolizes the Holy Spirit, and wine symbolizes salvation in Jesus Christ. Even when the Word of God is scarce, the Holy Spirit is still at work among people, and salvation is still available to all who desire it.

The fourth seal (6:7, 8)

The fourth seal opens and a pale horse appears. The Greek word for the horse's color is *chlóros*, denoting the ashen-gray color of a decomposing corpse. The rider's name is Death, and he is accompanied by Hades—the place of the dead. They are allowed to destroy people by the sword, famine, plague, and wild beasts over one-fourth of the earth. Noticeably, the actions of the fourth horseman comprise the actions of the previous three horsemen.

The fourth seal calls forth both pestilence and death. The graphic portrayal of this horseman provides a further warning to those who reject the gospel. The pale horse following the black one conveys the truth that spiritual famine of the Word of God typically results in spiritual death.

The good news, however, is that the power of Death and Hades is limited; they are given authority over only one-fourth of the earth. The beginning of Revelation provides the assurance that, by His own death and resurrection, Jesus has won the victory over Death and Hades—the two enemies of the human race. When the gospel is accepted, life is received as a gift. Death does not have power or authority over those who accept the gospel because Christ has the keys of Death and Hades (see Revelation 1:18).

The fifth seal (6:9-11)

The fifth seal scene portrays the souls of those who have been martyred for the sake of the gospel as residing underneath the altar. *Soul* in the Bible denotes the whole person (Genesis 2:7, KJV; Acts 2:41; 27:37, KJV). In this scene, the martyrs under the altar allude to the sacrificial blood poured at the base of the altar of sacrifice in the earthly sanctuary (Exodus 29:12; Leviticus 4:7; 8:15). The death of the martyrs is described here as pouring their sacrificial blood before God (2 Timothy 4:6).

John hears the martyrs crying to God for vindication against those who persecuted them: "How long, O Lord?" (Revelation 6:10) has been the cry of God's oppressed and persecuted people throughout history (cf. Psalm 79:5; Habakkuk 1:2). Thus, the martyrs' plea in the scene of the fifth seal represents the plea of God's suffering people throughout history, from the time of Abel until the time God judges and avenges "the blood of His servants" on their enemies (Revelation 19:2).

God responds to the plea of the martyred saints in two ways. First, they are given a white robe, signifying Christ's righteousness with which God covers those who are accepted by Christ (Revelation 3:18). It also represents the future reward of overcomers (verse 5). The martyred saints have received the assurance of salvation and eternal life, not because of their martyrdom but because of what God has done for them.

Second, the martyrs are told they will have to wait for a little while until their brothers in experience—those who must go through a similar martyrdom—are made complete. God

56

promised He will "avenge the blood of His servants" (Deuteronomy 32:43, NASB; cf. Psalm 79:10). In Revelation 8, God's judgments have already been poured out on "those who dwell on the earth" throughout Christian history (verse 13). The day is coming, however, when Christ will come in judgment to "those who do not obey the gospel of our Lord Jesus. These will pay the penalty of eternal destruction, away from the presence of the Lord and from the glory of His power, when He comes to be glorified in His saints on that day, and to be marveled at among all who have believed—for our testimony to you was believed" (2 Thessalonians 1:8–10). The fulfillment of this prophecy is the subject of the sixth seal scene.

While the fifth seal scene represents the experience of God's oppressed people throughout the Christian era, it may also apply to a specific period in history following the Middle Ages. During this period, millions of Christians were martyred because of their faithfulness to the Bible. The prophecies of Daniel speak of the enemy's power, described as a little horn "waging war with the saints and overpowering them" (Daniel 7:21, NASB; cf. verse 25). The question is raised: How long would such a situation last? The answer is that it would last for the prophetic period of 1,260 days, meaning 1,260 years (Revelation 12:6, 7). The opening of the sixth seal brings us to that point in time.

The sixth seal (6:12-17)

The breaking of the sixth seal by Christ the Lamb results in cosmic and cataclysmic signs, such as a darkening of the sun and the moon, a falling of meteors, a disastrous earthquake, and a convulsion of the sky. These cosmic signs are reminders that bring to mind the events foretold by Jesus in Matthew 24:29, 30, occurring at the conclusion of the tribulation of the Middle Ages. In the Old Testament, these events regularly accompany a manifestation of judgment.

These supernatural events will be witnessed at Christ's return to earth. Isaiah prophesied that the day of the Lord would come as "destruction from the Almighty" (Isaiah 13:6, NASB). Here John observes people from all walks of life, filled with fear, trying to hide themselves from the terrifying upheaval at Christ's coming. They ask the rocks and mountains to protect them from the wrath of God and the Lamb.

The day of divine wrath has finally come. It is with Christ's coming in power and glory that the prayers of the martyred saints underneath the altar in the fifth seal scene are ultimately answered (Revelation 6:9–11). The time has come for justice to be rendered, when Christ "comes to be glorified in His saints on that day, and to be marveled at among all who have believed" (2 Thessalonians 1:10, NASB).

The scene concludes with the rhetorical question of the terror-stricken wicked: "The great day of His wrath has come, and who is able to stand?" (Revelation 6:17). Their question echoes that of the people in Nahum, "Who can stand before His indignation? Who can endure the burning of His anger?" (Nahum 1:6, NASB), and Malachi, "Who can endure the day of His coming? And who can stand when He appears?" (Malachi 3:2, NASB). Revelation 7 clearly answers the question: those who will be able to stand in that day are the sealed people of God; those who are washed in the blood of the Lamb (verse 14).

CHAPTER 6

The Sealed People of God

Revelation 7 is inserted parenthetically between the sixth and seventh seals, yet it fits well in the sequence of the seals. The opening of the sixth seal brings us to Christ's second coming, and Revelation 7 answers the panic-stricken question of the wicked—"Who is able to stand?" (Revelation 6:17)—with a clear reply. Those who can stand are the sealed people of God.

The winds

Revelation 7 begins with four angels at "the four corners of the earth," restraining "the four winds" from destroying the earth, the sea, and the trees (verse 1). The expression "the four corners of the earth" is an ancient way of referring to the four points of the compass. This denotes the global significance of the scene.

In the Old Testament, winds symbolize destructive forces that God uses to execute judgments upon the wicked (Jeremiah 23:19, 20; Hosea 13:15). Jeremiah referred to the coming judgment against Jerusalem as a strong, scorching wind coming from the wilderness (Jeremiah 4:11–13). He also envisioned "the spirit [wind] of a destroyer" devastating Babylon (Jeremiah 51:1, 2, NASB). "The four winds" is a well-known concept in the Old Testament (Jeremiah 49:36). In vision, Daniel saw the "four winds of heaven were stirring up the great sea"

59

from which the four beasts emerged (Daniel 7:2, 3, NASB). The following passage from the book of Sirach shows how the Jews of John's day understood winds as a symbol of divine judgment:

> There are winds that have been created for vengeance,
> and in their anger they scourge heavily;
> in the time of consummation they will pour out their
> strength
> and calm the anger of their Maker.[1]

The blowing winds are associated with God's wrath in Revelation 6:17, and they take place during the time of "the great tribulation," mentioned later in the scene (Revelation 7:14). The blowing winds are another way to describe the seven last plagues, which are the fullness of God's wrath (Revelation 15:1). So the blowing winds represent the seven last plagues that will be poured out on the wicked just before the Second Coming. But for a certain period of time, divine intervention restrains these destructive forces from harming the earth. They are held in check while the sealing of God's people continues.

The sealing of God's people

John sees yet another angel coming from "the rising of the sun" (Revelation 7:2), which is an ancient designation of the east. This angel orders the four angels not to unleash the winds until the sealing of God's people is completed. In ancient times, sealing had a variety of meanings. Documents were sealed to validate their contents or to protect them from tampering. But the fundamental meaning of sealing was ownership. A seal impression on an object designated ownership. This is the symbolic meaning of sealing in the New Testament. According to Paul, the meaning of the seal is that "the Lord knows those who are His" (2 Timothy 2:19, NASB). Having the seal with the name of God on their foreheads signifies His ownership of the saved (Revelation 14:1).

Sealing in the New Testament denotes the identification of

those who are God's faithful people. God recognizes those who belong to Him and seals them with the Holy Spirit (2 Corinthians 1:21, 22; Ephesians 1:13, 14). The presence of the Holy Spirit is a sign of a genuine Christian—one who has washed his robes and made them white in the blood of the Lamb (see Revelation 7:14). To lose the Holy Spirit means to lose sealing: "Do not grieve the Holy Spirit of God, by whom you were sealed for the day of redemption" (Ephesians 4:30, NASB).

These passages show that the sealing of God's people in the New Testament is not limited to the time of the end. Sealing the faithful has been taking place throughout history. But the sealing of God's people reaches a climax at the time of the end. This will be a period of testing to distinguish between those who are on God's side and those who are on Satan's side. Those who side with the beast receive the mark of the beast on their foreheads or on their right hands (Revelation 13:16, 17). But those who worship God are sealed on their foreheads (Revelation 14:1).

The sealing described in Revelation 7 is the final ratification of those who belong to God. As such, the seal at the end time functions as a sign of protection. Those who have the seal of God on their foreheads are protected from the destructive forces of the seven last plagues. These are the ones who are able to stand on the great day of wrath (Revelation 7:3).

This concept goes back to Ezekiel 9:1–11, which is a passage about the destruction of Jerusalem before the Exile. In vision, the prophet saw a heavenly messenger with a writing case at his side. God ordered the messenger to go through the city and mark the foreheads of the faithful. The Lord then told the executioners to slay all those who did not have the mark on their foreheads. They were explicitly commanded not to touch those who were marked. The sign on the foreheads distinguished those who were on God's side from those who were unfaithful and idolatrous. The seal provided them with protection from the impending judgment.

Just as the marked Israelites were protected in Ezekiel's

vision, so God's sealed people are protected from the symbolic blowing of the eschatological winds. The sealing identifies them as God's people and protects them from the harmful effects of the seven last plagues. In this way, the question raised in Revelation 6:17 receives the ultimate answer: those who will be able to stand protected on the day of the divine wrath are the sealed people of God.

The sealed 144,000 (7:4)

As the vision continues, John hears the number of those who have been sealed as "144,000 sealed from every tribe of the sons of Israel" (Revelation 7:4). This shows that the sealing is completed and the destructive forces of the seven last plagues are to be unleashed. The 144,000 are about to go through the great tribulation.

Who are the 144,000? The context shows they are God's people living just before the end. Since Revelation is a symbolic book, 144,000 should not be taken as a literal number (cf. Revelation 1:1). In apocalyptic literature, numbers regularly have a symbolic meaning. The number 144,000 is made of 12 multiplied by 12, giving 144, and then is multiplied by 1,000. In the Bible, the number 12 functions as a symbol of the church. In the Old Testament, 12 is the number of tribes in Israel. In the New Testament, it is also the number of the church built upon the foundation of the 12 apostles (Ephesians 2:20). Thus, 144—12 tribes times 12 apostles—stands for the totality of God's end-time people, not a select group that is separated from the body of Christ.

Like the number 144,000, the twelve tribes of Israel are not literal for at least two reasons. First, the twelve tribes of Israel do not exist today. During the Assyrian conquest of the northern kingdom of Israel, the ten tribes were taken into captivity (2 Kings 17:6–23). They soon became integrated with other nations and disappeared. The two remaining tribes, Judah and Benjamin, were later taken into captivity in Babylon. They afterward returned to Palestine and were known as the Jews in the New Testament era. With the destruction of Jerusalem in

A.D. 70, the Jews were scattered throughout the Roman Empire, and even these two remaining tribes lost their national existence. Judaism today does not represent all twelve tribes.

Second, the list of the twelve tribes in Revelation 7 is not a regular list of the tribes of Israel. The tribes of Dan and Ephraim are missing, replaced by Joseph and Levi. This shows that Revelation 7 does not refer to the historical tribes of Israel. It is a theological list rather than a historical one.

The reason for the exclusion of Dan is because this tribe was the first to turn to idolatry (Judges 18:27–32). Later in Israel's history, the tribe of Dan became a center of idolatrous worship, competing with the temple worship in Jerusalem (1 Kings 12:28–31). This is also the reason for the exclusion of Ephraim. This Old Testament tribe symbolized apostasy and idolatry (2 Chronicles 30:1, 10; Hosea 4:17; 8:11).

These are the most likely reasons why Dan and Ephraim are excluded from the eschatological list of Israel's tribes in Revelation 7. The 144,000 are the true Israel that remains loyal to God. These members have washed their robes in the blood of the Lamb (Revelation 7:14). They are sealed and belong to God; they have not "been defiled with women" (Revelation 14:4)—women being a symbol for apostate churches. The unfaithfulness that characterized the tribes of Dan and Ephraim has no place among the sealed people of God. Only those who are faithful to God will be able to stand before God's throne and receive their eternal inheritance (Revelation 7:14–17).

The twelve tribes in Revelation 7 stand for the whole people of God. The church in the New Testament is referred to in terms of the twelve tribes of Israel (James 1:1). Paul calls the church "the Israel of God" (Galatians 6:16, NASB); Christians are Abraham's seed and the heirs of the covenant promises (Galatians 3:29). The 144,000, consisting of 12,000 from each of the 12 tribes, symbolize God's people right before the end. This is the group that is sealed and readied to enter the great tribulation of the seven last plagues, fully protected by the seal of God on their foreheads.

In describing God's end-time people standing on the threshold of the great tribulation, Revelation uses the language of warfare. The 144,000 are portrayed as an army modeled after ancient Israel going to war. Their number is comprised of 12 multiplied by 12 multiplied by 1,000. In Old Testament war scenes, 1,000 (Hebrew *eleph*) is a basic military unit (Numbers 31:3–6; 1 Samuel 8:12; 22:7). The 144,000 consist of 12 tribes; each has 12 military units of 1,000 for a total of 12,000 soldiers. The 12 tribes, thus, give a total of 144,000 soldiers. So the symbolic number 144,000 symbolizes an army of 144 military units ready to go to battle against Satan and his army of 200 million (Revelation 9:16). Revelation 19:18 shows that Satan's army is also organized into military units of 1,000 (the Greek word *chiliarchos* denotes a commander of 1,000 soldiers; also in Revelation 6:15).

Thus, 144,000 is a symbolic reference to the militant church, organized like ancient Israel into military units about to enter the final and greatest battle in the world's history: the battle of Armageddon (cf. Revelation 16:16). While the symbolic seal identifies the 144,000 as those who are on God's side in the final conflict, it also protects them from the righteous judgments of God that are about to fall on the wicked.

The great multitude (7:9-17)

Having heard the number of God's sealed people, John then sees a great multitude that nobody can count, from every nation, tribe, people, and tongue. They are all dressed in white, standing before the Lamb and the throne and praising God and the Lamb for their salvation. Many Christians assume that, in contrast to the 144,000, the great multitude is God's people from all ages.

But Revelation 7 does not support such an assertion. John makes it clear that the great multitude is also the last generation of God's people. Notice that in Revelation 7:9, John sees the great multitude in white robes before the throne of God. Later one of the elders explains to him that those in white robes are the ones who have come out of the great tribulation (verse 14). They have washed their robes in the blood of the Lamb and now stand before the throne of God, serving Him day and night in His temple (verse 15). This shows that the great multitude is the last generation of God's people—the ones who will go through the great tribulation of the seven last plagues.

As we interpret this group, a literary feature of Revelation must be kept in mind. This feature is characterized by an "I heard" and "I saw" pattern. Often, John hears about something in the vision. Later he sees what he has heard about through a different symbol and from a different perspective. For instance, in Revelation 5:5, John hears that the Lion from the tribe of Judah has overcome. But what he sees a few moments later is the slain Lamb (verse 6). The Lion and the Lamb are both symbols of Christ: the Lion shows what Christ did, and the Lamb shows how He did it.

This is the situation we find in Revelation 7. John hears that the number of God's sealed people is 144,000. But they appear to him as a great, incalculable crowd. This shows that the 144,000 and the great multitude are one and the same group; they are God's end-time people in different times and circumstances.

It seems clear that the 144,000 are portrayed as the church militant, organized into 144 military divisions, entering the final war of this world's history. The great multitude, on the other hand, is portrayed as the church triumphant, coming out of that war and celebrating the victory. The war is over, and they are no longer organized into military divisions. They appear to John as a multitude that is impossible to count. The reason they cannot be counted is not because of their large number, but because they appear to him as a crowd impossible to count in contrast to the 144,000, who can be easily numbered.

Nowhere in the Bible does it say that at the time of the end God will have a final generation of saints who reach a level of holiness unattainable by those who lived before them. The 144,000 are not a select group, separated from the rest of God's people and granted special privileges unavailable to the rest of the redeemed. The 144,000 are not the only ones who were persecuted nor are they the first to have been sealed. Furthermore, they are not the only ones redeemed nor the first to be found blameless before the throne.

In God's kingdom, all of His people are, without distinction, promised white robes (Revelation 3:4, 5; 6:11; 19:8). This makes them all equal before God with no clans, ranks, or privileges available to some and not to others.

---

1. Sirach 39:28, RSV.

Remember —
It's all about Jesus!

The Seven Trumpets

Revelation 8:2 begins a new vision with seven angels blowing trumpets. As the trumpets sound, a chain of events is unleashed on the earth. In dealing with this section, it is important to remember a special literary feature that is repeated several times in the book: the interlude. As John the revelator begins a new description of the vision, he suddenly interrupts his commentary by inserting another scene with different content.

The prayers of the saints and seven trumpets

The first interlude of Revelation 8 is situated in verses 3–5. Verse 2 describes seven angels with trumpets standing before God, and it is not until verse 6 that they are commissioned to blow their trumpets. Between are verses 3 to 5, depicting a scene that takes place in the sanctuary setting.

In Revelation 8:2, John observes seven angels with trumpets, ready to herald the judgments that will fall upon the earth's inhabitants. Before the angels blow the trumpets, another unspecified angel appears holding a golden censer. He stands upon the altar,[1] which is evidently the altar of sacrifice. The altar of sacrifice was located in the outer court of the temple, and in biblical typology, the outer court stands for the earth (cf. Revelation 11:2). This shows that the scene in Revelation 8:3–5 begins on earth.

At the altar, the angel is given "much incense" (Revelation 8:3). He takes the incense into the Holy Place and offers it with the prayers of the saints on the golden altar before the throne of God. "The smoke of the incense with the prayers of the saints ascended before God from the hand of the angel" (verse 4). Afterward, the angel fills the censer with fire from the golden altar and hurls it to the earth. Throwing the censer filled with fire produces "thunder and sounds and flashes of lightning and an earthquake" (verse 5). This is the signal for the seven angels to blow their trumpets.

This scene reflects the daily services in the earthly temple.[2] After the sacrificial lamb had been placed on the altar of sacrifice, the blood was poured out at the base of the altar. The appointed priest would take a golden censer and fill it with coals from the altar. He would then take incense into the temple and offer it on the golden altar in the Holy Place. Having offered the incense, the priest would come out of the temple and throw the censer down on the pavement between the altar of sacrifice and the entrance of the temple, producing a very loud noise. At that moment, seven priests blew trumpets, marking the end of the daily services.

The symbolic act in Revelation 8:3–5—replicating the daily services in the earthly temple—gives insight into the meaning of the seven trumpets. The incense the angel burns on the golden altar represents the prayers of God's people (Revelation 5:8; cf. Psalm 141:2). This incense originated from the altar of sacrifices, underneath which, in the fifth seal, the blood of the martyred saints petitions God for judgment "on those who dwell on earth" (Revelation 6:10). This shows that the incense the angel ministers before God represents the prayers of God's suffering people. Now, judgment will fall on "those who dwell on the earth" in answer to the prayers of the slain saints, found in the fifth seal scene (Revelation 8:13).

The seven trumpets refer to God's intervention in history in response to the prayers of His oppressed people. They sound

God's judgment against those who have harmed His people. Yet they are not God's final word to the wicked. While punitive in intent, these judgments are mixed with mercy. Their purpose is to warn the earth's inhabitants before the day of judgment, offering them salvation before it is too late.

To what time in history do the seven trumpets refer? The daily services of the earthly temple provide a clue to the beginning of the seven trumpets' sounding. In the earthly temple, the trumpets sounded after the sacrifice had been offered on the altar. Following this pattern, the sounding of the seven trumpets should begin after Jesus' death on the cross. They occur while Jesus intercedes in heaven (verses 3–5) and the gospel is preached (Revelation 10:8–11:14). This means the trumpets concern the Christian age—from the Cross to the Second Coming—until the seventh trumpet sounds and God establishes His kingdom (Revelation 11:15–18).

The trumpets cover the same span of history as the seven seals. The two series correspond both structurally and sequentially. Sequentially, the seals and the trumpets both begin in the first century, following the death of Jesus on the cross and His ascension into heaven. The conclusion of both series brings us to the time of the end. Structurally, the two series are subdivided into groups of four and three with interludes between the sixth and seventh segments. While the interlude between the sixth and seventh seals describes God's end-time people, the interlude between the sixth and seventh trumpets describes their experience and role during the end time.

The difference between the two series lies in their focus. While the seals primarily concern those who profess to be God's people, however unfaithful they are to the gospel, the trumpets exclusively concern those who do not profess to belong to God. Yet God wants both groups to be saved. He wants to win them over before the door of salvation is closed.

The angel with the scroll (10:1-7)
During the interlude between the sixth and seventh trumpets, John sees an angel of magnificent appearance descending from

heaven. He is referred to as "another strong angel" to distinguish him from the seven angels who blew the trumpets (Revelation 10:1). The description of the angel resembles the description of Christ found in Revelation 1 (cf. verses 12–16). These descriptions are symbolic images that the Bible uses in referring to God.

In his hand, the angel holds an open little scroll, containing the description of the time of the end and the experience of God's people in the world during the last days (Revelation 12–22). Christ has disclosed these things to God's people via the angel to prepare them for the final crisis of this world's history (cf. Revelation 1:1).

Time no longer (10:5-7)

With a solemn voice, the angel swears by the Eternal One who created the heavens, the earth, and all that is in them, declaring that "there will no longer be time" (Revelation 10:6). Furthermore, during the sounding of the seventh angel, the mystery of God will be completed, as was revealed to His servants the prophets (verse 7).

This scene points to Daniel 12:4–10. Daniel was ordered to seal up the words of the scroll until the time of the end. Afterward, there is a question regarding how long it would be before the persecution of the saints is over and the prophesied events take place. In response, the heavenly messenger raises his hands toward heaven and swears an oath by the One who lives forever that the persecution of God's people will last "a time, times, and half a time" (Daniel 12:7, NASB), then the end will come. Until then, God's people must wait patiently (verse 10).

Revelation 10 clearly echoes Daniel 12, with the exception of the phrase "there will no longer be time," which replaces the phrase "a time, times, and half a time" from Daniel. "A time, times, and half a time" is a symbolic designation of the prophetic period of 1,260 years, referring to the Middle Ages when God's people were persecuted by the antichrist power. The end would come after this prophetic period.

In Revelation 6:10, there is the perennial plea of God's

oppressed people: "How long, O Lord, holy and true, will You not judge and avenge our blood on those who dwell on earth?" They are told to wait for a short time (verse 11). Now in Revelation 10:6, God's people are assured, by means of a divine oath, that "there will no longer be time." God has heard the plea of His people found in the fifth seal. The end-time events will soon unfold.

Although the time of the end prophesied by Daniel is set in motion, the angel warns John that the end is not yet here. It is at the sound of the seventh trumpet that the end will come and the mystery of God will be complete, which is all in accordance with the proclamations of the prophets (verse 7) and Daniel, in particular.

The mystery referred to by the angel encompasses the whole purpose of God: to establish His eternal kingdom, symbolized by the sealed scroll of Revelation 5 that will be unsealed at the coming of Christ. At this time, as Paul stated, God will "bring to light the things hidden in the darkness and disclose the motives of men's hearts" (1 Corinthians 4:5, NASB). But at the Second Coming, the fullness of this mystery will be revealed to the entire universe (Revelation 20:11–15).

The two witnesses (11:3-6)

Now the scene shifts from the angel to two witnesses who epitomize the bitter Christian experience during the prophetic 1,260 days. John describes them in terms of several Old Testament personalities. First, they are characterized as "the two olive trees and the two lampstands standing before the Lord" (Revelation 11:4). Here John points to Zechariah's vision of the lampstand between the two olive trees (Zechariah 4:2, 3). Zechariah was told that the two olive trees represented "the two anointed ones" standing by the Lord of the earth (verse 14, NASB), specifically Joshua, the high priest, and Zerubbabel, the governor of Judea. Resembling the roles of Joshua and Zerubbabel, the two witnesses are portrayed in priestly and royal terms.

Next, John portrays them as Elijah and Moses (Revelation

11:5, 6). Elijah closed up the heavens so that it would not rain for three and a half years (equaling 1,260 days; 1 Kings 17; cf. Luke 4:25) and brought down fire from heaven on soldiers who came to arrest him (2 Kings 1:9–14). In the same manner, the two witnesses send fire from their mouths on their enemies, shutting up the heavens so that it will not rain during the 1,260 days (or three and a half years). Just as Moses turned water into blood and struck the land of Egypt with all kinds of plagues (Exodus 7–11), the two witnesses also have authority to turn water into blood and strike the earth with plagues.

Who are these two witnesses? Their portrayal points to God's people as they bear witness to the Bible and to the gospel in the world. Revelation 11:8 shows that the two witnesses are one entity rather than two (the Greek reads, "The dead body of them"). It is appropriate to see the two witnesses as the people of God in their royal and priestly roles, preaching the Bible as the Word of God (cf. Revelation 1:6; 5:10).[3] It is because of their faithfulness to the Bible that God's people suffered through the Middle Ages during the prophetic period of the 1,260 days or forty-two months (Revelation 6:9; 12:6, 13, 14).

The killing of the two witnesses (11:7-10)

After the two witnesses have completed their work during the 1,260 days, "the beast [symbolizing political power (Revelation 13; 17:3–8)] coming up from the abyss will make war with them and will conquer them and kill them" (Revelation 11:7). Since the abyss is the abode of Satan (Luke 8:31; 2 Peter 2:4), this beast is controlled and backed by Satan, specifically the dominant political power at the end of the 1,260 days. Seventh-day Adventists have rightly identified the killing of the two witnesses with the atheist assault on the Bible and the abolition of religion during the French Revolution. Both events transpired at the conclusion of the prophetic 1,260-day period.

The two witnesses lie dead and are publicly exposed "on the street of the great city" (Revelation 11:8). In Revelation, "the great city" often refers to end-time Babylon, a power at odds with God's people in the final conflict.

In Revelation 11, the great city is a territory governed by the beast arising from the abyss at the end of the prophetic 1,260 days. This territory has the spiritual characteristics of the great biblical cities that stood in opposition to God. It possesses the wickedness and moral degradation of Sodom (Genesis 19:4–11), the atheistic arrogance of Egypt (Exodus 5:2), and the rebelliousness of Jerusalem, "where also their Lord was crucified" (Revelation 11:8). Likewise, this great symbolic city kills the Christian church and the Bible.

The body of the witnesses lies exposed and unburied for three and a half days, mirroring the time Jesus spent in the tomb. Their death causes great joy among "those who dwell on the earth" (Revelation 11:10), which is a clear reference to the wicked (Revelation 6:10; 8:13; 13:8, 14; 17:2). They are celebrating because "these two prophets tormented those who dwell on the earth" (Revelation 11:10). The Word of God always troubles the conscience of those who hear it but are unwilling to surrender.

The resurrection of the two witnesses (11:11-14)

Three and a half days later, God breathes life into the two witnesses and resurrects them. He also makes them stand erect. This entire scene, however, recalls Ezekiel's vision of the valley of dry bones (Ezekiel 37:1–10), which was a prophecy of Israel's restoration after the Babylonian exile. Israel was perceived by its enemies to have been defeated and killed. But in his vision, God ordered Ezekiel to prophesy so breath could enter the dry bones. The breath entered the dead bodies, and they came to life and stood on their feet.

Historically, one of the outcomes of the French Revolution was a great revival of interest in the Bible, manifested, in particular, by the establishment of the great Bible societies and numerous missionary societies. These were founded to spread the gospel and fulfilled the prophecy of the two witnesses brought back to life. Like never before, the stage was set for the widespread preaching of the gospel.

The ascension of the resurrected witnesses is accompanied

by a great earthquake that strikes a tenth of the great city and kills seven thousand people. A tenth in the Bible symbolizes the smallest part of a whole;[4] and the seven thousand people killed represent the totality of the hardened unbelievers.[5]

The rest of the people are filled with fear and give glory to God. This brings to mind the conversion of King Nebuchadnezzar, who gave glory to God after experiencing divine judgment (Daniel 4:34–37). The word *fear* and the phrase *gave glory to God* sound like a response to the appeal of the first angel in Revelation 14:7: "Fear God, and give Him glory." This suggests, as a result of the vindication and exaltation of the two witnesses and the earthquake that shook the great city, there are some who will accept the gospel and find faith in Christ.

While the testimony of the two witnesses applies historically to the Middle Ages, it also applies to the context of the French Revolution. But its significance for God's end-time people goes beyond this temporal and geographical location. It shows that, as in the past, God has people who are faithful in bearing witness to the gospel in today's world. He uses them as He used Moses during the Exodus, Elijah during Israel's apostasy, and Joshua and Zerubbabel during the postexilic period.

---

1. The Greek text shows that the angel stood *upon* the altar rather than *at* the altar, as suggested by other translations. See Ranko Stefanovic, "The Angel at the Altar (Revelation 8:3-5): A Case Study on Intercalations in Revelation," *Andrews University Seminary Studies* 44, no. 1 (Spring 2006): 79–94.

2. See Mishnah Tamid, 4:1–5:6. See Emil Schürer, *The History of the Jewish People in the Age of Jesus Christ*, 2nd ed. (London: T & T Clark, 1979), 2:299–308.

3. This twofold interpretation is also in Ellen White's writings. While she interpreted the two witnesses as representing the Old and New Testament scriptures (*The Great Controversy* [Nampa, ID: Pacific Press®, 2005], 267), she also talks about the church prophesying in sackcloth during troublous times (*Testimonies for the Church* [Mountain View, CA: Pacific Press®, 1948], 4:594, 595).

4. Jacques B. Doukhan, *Secrets of Daniel* (Hagerstown, MD: Review and Herald®, 2000), 23n7.

5. G. K. Beale, *The Book of Revelation*, New International Greek Testament Commentary (Grand Rapids, MI: Eerdmans, 1999), 603.

CHAPTER 8

Satan, a Defeated Enemy

Revelation 12 describes a new vision that begins the eschatological portion of Revelation. While the first half of Revelation describes the historic struggles of the church in a hostile world, the primary focus of the second half of the book is on the time of the end and the final events leading to Christ's return. From now on, Revelation focuses on the contents of the open scroll (Revelation 10).

The woman (12:1, 2)

In vision, John sees a great sign in heaven. Something special and remarkable is shown here (cf. Revelation 12:3; 15:1). The Greek word *sémeion* (sign) denotes a symbolic presentation of a real object. This sign is a woman arrayed with the sun, standing on the moon, and having a garland of twelve stars on her head. She is in labor and about to give birth to a child.

A woman in the Bible is a symbol of God's people, whether faithful to God or apostate. In the Old Testament, Israel, as God's covenant people, is often referred to as the wife of God (Isaiah 54:5; Jeremiah 3:20). When Israel was faithful to its covenant with God, it was called a pure and faithful woman. On the other hand, apostate and idolatrous Israel was portrayed as a prostitute. This concept is also carried into the New

Testament and applied to the church (cf. 2 Corinthians 11:2; Ephesians 5:25–32). In Revelation, God's faithful people are represented as a faithful woman (Revelation 19:7, 8; 22:17), while a prostitute symbolizes the apostate and unfaithful (chaps. 17; 18).

The picture of a beautifully adorned woman in travail brings to mind several Old Testament passages. For one, it echoes the portrayal of Solomon's bride, who is "as beautiful as the full moon, as pure as the sun" (Song of Solomon 6:10, NASB). It also reflects the passages depicting Israel as a travailing woman (Isaiah 26:17, 18; 66:7–9; Jeremiah 4:31; Micah 4:10). But above all, the portrayal of a woman enduring the pangs of giving birth to the Messiah is an allusion to Genesis 3:15. Revelation 12 shows the fulfillment of God's promise to redeem fallen humanity through the woman's offspring.

The remarkable woman of Revelation 12 stands as a symbol for the church in both the Old and New Testaments. This reality is expressed through her portrayal—clothed with the sun and standing on the moon. The sun, as the source of light, stands for the gospel (2 Corinthians 4:6; cf. John 8:12; 12:46), and the moon reflects the light of the sun. The woman stands on the revelation of the Old Testament that reflects the light of the gospel.[1] The twelve stars on her head stand for the twelve tribes of Israel as well as the twelve apostles. In this part of the vision (Revelation 12:1–5), the woman represents Old Testament Israel bringing the Messiah into the world. But in verses 6, 13–17, she represents the Christian church.

The dragon (12:3-6)

In opposition to the woman is the dragon, or Satan, who is the serpent of Genesis 3. His seven heads represent the kingdoms in history through which he has worked to oppose God's plans and purpose in the world and to oppress God's people (Revelation 17:9–11). The ten horns on his heads symbolize political authorities (verse 12). The seven crowns on the dragon's heads refer to Satan's false claim of lordship over this world (cf. Luke 4:6). This imagery reveals Satan standing behind the Roman

Empire as he tried to destroy the long-awaited Messiah, Jesus Christ.

Satan is a real enemy, not an imaginary figure. Since God announced that there would come the One born from "the woman" who would crush the serpent's head (Genesis 3:15), Satan has waited for the Promised Child to be born in order to destroy Him. Although Satan desires to kill this Child, he cannot because the Child is taken to heaven (Revelation 12:5), referring to Christ's exaltation to the heavenly throne (Ephesians 1:20–22; 1 Peter 3:21, 22). The exaltation of Christ serves to introduce the subsequent scene (Revelation 12:7–12); an event that ultimately resulted in the permanent expulsion of Satan from heaven (verse 10).

As Christ is taken to heaven, to the throne of God, the woman, representing the church, finds divine protection in the desert during the prophetic time period of 1,260 days. During this time, she waits for the return of Christ and the establishment of His eternal kingdom.

War in heaven (12:7-12)

Revelation 12:7–12 transitions to a new scene in the story. The depiction reveals that at the ascension of Christ and His exaltation to the heavenly throne, a war erupted in heaven. Michael and his angels fought against Satan and his angels. Michael (a name meaning "who is like God?") is the commander of the heavenly host. Elsewhere in the Bible, he is identified as the chief prince (Daniel 10:13, 21; 12:1) and the archangel (Jude 9). Thus, the biblical information leads to the conclusion that Michael is an eschatological name for Christ.

Here in Revelation 12, Christ leads the heavenly army in fighting Satan. Satan and his angels fight back but lose. As a result, Satan and his forces are expelled from heaven and sent to earth (verse 9). When did this war in heaven and the expulsion of Satan and his angels take place? Clues are given in the anthem heard in heaven following Satan's dismissal (verses 10–12):

- "Now the salvation and the power and the kingdom of

our God and the authority of His Christ have come" (verse 10). The kingdom of God and the authority of Christ are established after the death of Jesus on the cross.

- "The accuser of our brothers has been cast down, the one who accuses them before our God day and night" (verse 10). Satan's accusation could not have taken place at the beginning of the great controversy because humans were not yet created. The Old Testament often pictures Satan accusing God's people before God (Job 1; 2; Zechariah 3).
- Having been expelled from heaven, Satan realizes he has a short time left (Revelation 12:12). He recognizes this after Jesus' death on the cross.
- After his expulsion, Satan starts persecuting the church during the prophetic period of 1,260 days (verse 13). This period refers to the Middle Ages, starting in A.D. 538 and concluding with the French Revolution and the capture of Pope Pius VI by Napoleon's general Berthier in A.D. 1798.

All this shows that the war and expulsion of Satan from heaven portrayed in Revelation 12:7–9 took place after Jesus' death on the cross and His subsequent ascension to heaven.

Satan was first expelled from heaven at the beginning of his rebellion against God's government. He wanted to take Heaven's throne in order to be "like the Most High" (Isaiah 14:14, NASB). He stood in open revolt against God but was defeated and cast down to earth. By deceiving Adam, Satan usurped the rule and dominion of this earth (Luke 4:6). Jesus referred to him as "the ruler of this world" (John 12:31, NASB; 14:30; 16:11).

But after Satan's expulsion, he still had access to heaven. The book of Job portrays him as attending the heavenly assembly before God and making accusations against Job (Job 1:6–12; 2:1–7). Similarly, Zechariah saw him in a vision, accusing Joshua the high priest before the heavenly court (Zechariah 3:1, 2).

The situation changed with Jesus' death on the cross. Dominion over the earth was transferred from Satan to Jesus. This transfer of authority obviously did not take place without resistance from Satan, who once again stood in open revolt against God. At this point, Satan and his associates were forever expelled from heaven.

With Satan's expulsion, "the kingdom of our God and the authority of His Christ have come" (Revelation 12:10). Since that time, Satan and the fallen angels have been confined to the earth as a prison, until they receive their punishment (2 Peter 2:4; Jude 6). Satan no longer has access to the heavenly courts and can no longer accuse God's people in heaven.

While the fate of Satan was decided with his expulsion from heaven, his defeat is not yet complete. He still claims lordship over the earth, which is why Heaven gives this warning: "Woe to the earth and the sea, for the devil has come down to you, having great anger, knowing that he has little time" (Revelation 12:12). The reference to the earth and the sea points to the global dimension of this warning. Particularly significant in this regard is Revelation 13, where Satan's two associates arise out of the earth and the sea to cause the earth's inhabitants to side with Satan in the final crisis.

War on earth (12:13-16)

Satan could not harm Christ, but he knows how dear the church is to Him. So he now turns against the church that represents Christ on earth. But the woman (the church) is given "two wings of a great eagle" to fly to the wilderness, where she is cared for by God for a period of "a time and times and half a time" (Revelation 12:14), or 1,260 days (verse 6).

This language echoes Israel's Exodus from Egypt (Exodus 19:4). As God cared for Israel during its wilderness years (Deuteronomy 8:15–18), He now cares for the church in the wilderness during the prophetic period of 1,260 days (A.D. 538–1798). During this period of time, God's people suffered persecution by the antichrist power (Revelation 13:5). The established church of western Europe persecuted those who chose to follow the Bible's teachings rather than tradition. Millions of Christians were martyred for their faithfulness to the gospel. During that time, God's faithful people found a refuge in isolated places to escape persecution and the corrupt influences of the institutional church.

In an effort to destroy the woman, "the serpent poured out of his mouth water like a river after the woman, in order to make her flooded by the water" (Revelation 12:15). This torrent of water from the serpent's mouth is reminiscent of the serpent's deceptive words in the Garden of Eden (Genesis 3:1–5). In the same manner, Satan is trying to destroy God's people with a flood of false teaching. In the Old Testament, a flood of water is often used as a symbol of the enemies of God's people attacking and destroying them (Psalms 69:1, 2; 124:2–5; Isaiah 8:7, 8; Jeremiah 47:2).

Thus, the flood of water poured out of the dragon's mouth has two meanings: persecution and false teachings. These are the weapons Satan used against God's people during the prophetic period of 1,260 days in the medieval era. Providentially, however, the earth rescues the woman by swallowing the waters sent forth by the dragon (Revelation 12:16). Once again, John uses the language of the Exodus. Just as the earth swallowed the Egyptians who were pursuing the Israelites (Exodus 15:12), so the friendly earth swallows the torrent of persecution and false teachings that the dragon used to destroy the woman.

Satan's attack on the remnant (12:17)

Up until now, the dragon has not been able to destroy the woman, but he does not give up. He regroups to "make war with the remnant of her offspring, the ones keeping the commandments of God and having the testimony of Jesus" (Revelation 12:17). This passage serves as an introduction to Revelation 13, where Satan prepares for the final battle against God's end-time people. He retreats to prepare for his last attack against God's end-time people and chooses the help of two allies: the sea beast (Revelation 13:1–10) and the earth beast (verses 11–18). Together, these three form an unholy triumvirate to fight the final battle against Christ and His faithful remnant.

The term *remnant* in the Old Testament describes those who have survived destruction to continue as God's faithful people (Isaiah 10:20–22; 11:11, 12; Jeremiah 23:3; Zephaniah 3:13). Throughout Old Testament times, as the majority of the nation of Israel apostatized, there were people who remained faithful to God (cf. 1 Kings 19:18). John employs the word *remnant* in reference to the Christians who remained faithful to God in the churches of Thyatira and Sardis (Revelation 2:24; 3:4). And now John uses the same word to say that at the end of time, as the majority of people in the world side with Satan and his allies, there will be a people who remain faithful to Christ.

This end-time remnant will have two characteristics. The first is its obedience to God's commandments. Revelation 13 shows at the end of time that the first four commandments of the Decalogue will be central to the end-time conflict. Since the issue in the final crisis will concern worship—regarding whom and when we are to worship—the fourth commandment will become a test of loyalty and obedience to God (cf. Revelation 14:7).

The second characteristic of the end-time remnant is that they have the testimony of Jesus. This characteristic is linked with "the spirit of prophecy" (Revelation 19:10; cf. Revelation 22:9). The expression "the spirit of prophecy" was used in John's day to designate the Holy Spirit speaking through prophets, and the phrase "the testimony of Jesus" refers to Jesus bearing witness to Himself through His prophets (Revelation 19:10). Satan will make every effort to deceive and destroy the remnant, but Revelation shows that God's faithful people will have the prophetic gift to guide them through these hard times.

Satan's end-time strategy

At this point, there is a shift in Satan's strategy for trying to win people over to his side. Understanding his scheme will help us to avoid his deceptive snare. Throughout history, Satan has been attacking the church by means of persecution and coercion. As he begins his final attack against the end-time remnant, his strategy changes from coercion to deception. This shift in strategy corresponds to the transition from the historical to the eschatological focus of Revelation. One might observe that the word *deceive* does not occur at all in the historical section of Revelation (chaps. 4–11), but it is used regularly in the eschatological section (chaps. 12–20) to describe Satan's end-time activities in preparing for the final crisis.

Endeavoring to win the allegiance of the world, Satan will launch a great counterfeit of the true God and His efforts to save humankind. Revelation 13 describes this assault as the work of the dragon, the beast from the sea, and the beast from the earth; a trio whose mission is the destruction of the Trinity (Revelation 1:4–6). From here on out, the members of this satanic triad are inseparably associated in their quest to deceive the world and turn people away from God (Revelation 16:13, 14; 19:20; 20:10).

---

1. Leon Morris, *Revelation*, Tyndale New Testament Commentaries, rev. ed. (Grand Rapids, MI: Eerdmans, 1987), 152.

CHAPTER

Satan and His Two Allies

In Revelation 13, John's vision shifts to a monstrous beast coming out of the sea. In the Bible, the beast is a symbol of a political power, and the sea symbolizes stormy social and political conditions, out of which evil powers emerge to attack God's people (cf. Daniel 7:2, 3).

Description of the beast (13:1-4)

John describes the beast as he views it emerging from the water. Surfacing first are ten horns and upon them are crowns of political authority. These ten horns find their counterpart in the ten horns of Daniel 7, which symbolizes the division of the Roman Empire and the nations that sprang up in the wake of its demise (Daniel 7:24).[1] Appearing next are seven heads with blasphemous names on them. The heads of the beast are notable powers used by Satan to persecute God's people throughout history (Revelation 17:9–11). The blasphemous names point to the divine titles the beast claims. Though the crowns have shifted from the heads to the horns, this description of the beast mirrors the depiction of the dragon in Revelation 12:3, which shows that this power is a true representative of the dragon.

As the beast eventually steps out of the water, John sees that its parts resemble a leopard, a bear, and a lion. Thus, the beast combines the characteristics of the four beasts coming out of the sea in Daniel 7:2–8, representing four world kingdoms: Babylon, Media-Persia, Greece, and Rome (verse 17). But John lists them in reverse order, showing that the sea beast is the same as the fourth terrifying beast of Daniel 7, which appeared as a successor of the three kingdoms that came before it (Daniel 7:7). The fact that the ten horns of the sea beast have royal crowns shows that the power represented by the sea beast appears in history after the demise of the Roman Empire, which was a time when the resulting nations sprang up and exercised political authority.

Power and authority are delegated to the beast by Satan: "The dragon gave him his power and his throne and great authority" (Revelation 13:2). Here is an enthronement scene that copies the enthronement of Christ in Revelation 5. Just as the Father has given His throne and authority to Christ (cf. Revelation 2:27; 3:21), so the dragon gives his throne and authority to the beast, investing him as his coregent and representative on earth. This affirms what was stated before—this symbolic sea beast is the second member of the false trinity. This ally of Satan wants to take the place of Jesus Christ in the minds and the hearts of the people.

John goes on to say that, at some point in history, one of the beast's heads gets a deadly wound, causing the death of the beast. But the mortal wound is eventually healed, and the beast is restored to life (Revelation 13:3). This mirrors the death and resurrection of Jesus Christ; in Greek, the same word for slaying the beast is used for the death of Christ the Lamb (Revelation 5:6). These three phases of the sea beast's existence are defined in Revelation 17:8 in terms of the beast who "was, and is not, and is about to come." This descriptor is the antithesis of the divine title: "who is, and who was, and who is coming" (Revelation 1:4; cf. Revelation 4:8).

The resurrection of the beast prompts amazement among the earth's inhabitants. In admiration, they worship both the beast and the dragon standing behind the beast, saying, "Who is like the beast, and who is able to wage war with him?" (Revelation 13:4). This implies that no one is like him or able to do these things. "Who is like the beast?" stands in contrast to "Who is like God?" (Exodus 15:11; Psalm 35:10; Micah 7:18) The phrase "Who is like God?" is the Hebrew meaning of *Michael*, who is the same Michael who defeats the dragon in heaven (Revelation 12:7). Given this understanding, it seems clear that the beast is an end-time ally of Satan who accomplishes his deceptive mission by posing as the counterpart of Jesus Christ and His saving ministry.

Activities of the beast (13:5-10)

The beast's activities are described as the mouth speaking great things and blasphemies during the prophetic period of forty-two months. These activities of the beast echo the activities of the antidivine power of the little horn coming from the fourth beast in Daniel 7. The parallels between the two visions show that Daniel 7 and Revelation 13 deal with the same earthly power.

First, the sea beast's blasphemies involve the name of God (Revelation 13:5, 6). In the New Testament, blasphemy denotes a claim of equality with God (John 10:33; Matthew 26:63–65) or God's prerogatives (Mark 2:7). The sea beast of Revelation 13 claims the titles of God and the prerogatives that belong only to God.

Second, the sea beast's blasphemies are directed against God's tabernacle and those who dwell in it. The dwelling of God is the sanctuary in heaven where Christ ministers on behalf of His people. The sea beast denies Christ's mediatorial work in the heavenly sanctuary by substituting it with a human system of salvation and forgiveness of sins.

What earthly power does the sea beast represent? The text shows that this power is the successor of the Roman Empire and exercises its authority and power during the prophetic forty-two months, or 1,260 days—the same period as the little horn's activities in Daniel 7. The only period that aptly fits this time frame is the Middle Ages, during which the established church of western Europe exercised political and religious oppression. Thus, Revelation 13 is a prophecy of the major apostasy in the Christian church's history.

The rise of the medieval church to power and dominance was gradual. By A.D. 538, the Christian church had established itself as an ecclesiastical power and continued to dominate the Western world throughout medieval times. This date marks the beginning of the prophetic period of forty-two months, or 1,260 days, symbolizing years. During this period, the state church of western Europe claimed that the pope was its head, with the position and prerogatives of God. These claims were reiterated in modern times by the statement of Pope Leo XIII: "We [the popes] hold upon this earth the place of God Almighty."[2]

In addition, the atoning ministry of Christ in the heavenly sanctuary was replaced by the claims of the priesthood to forgive sins. All those who insisted on living by the Bible rather than the state religion experienced persecution and martyrdom. Historians believe that millions of Christians were martyred for their faithfulness to the Bible's teachings. Although in modern times of ecumenism and religious tolerance such statements are regarded as harsh and unfair, the present cannot erase the historical facts and reality.

In 1798, Napoleon's army inflicted a deadly wound upon the beast by capturing Pope Pius VI, marking the demise of the papacy and the conclusion of the 1,260-day prophetic period. The state-instituted religion and God-centered theology that had dominated the Western world for centuries was replaced by the human-centered and materialistic outlook of the modern world.

But Revelation 13 goes on to say that the religiopolitical power Satan used during the Middle Ages, seriously wounded by the French Revolution, would rise again and exercise its oppressive power over the world. The healing of the beast's mortal wound will fill the world's inhabitants with awe and admiration: "And all those who dwell on the earth will worship him, whose names are not written in the book of life of the Lamb slain from the foundation of the world" (Revelation 13:8).

And what will cause the healing of the beast's mortal wound? The answer is found in the description of another earthly power appearing on the world scene. A power that will play a key role in reviving the medieval oppressive authority and will force its acceptance by the world's inhabitants.

The beast from the earth

This second beast comes from the earth—the same earth that in Revelation 12:14–16 saved the woman from the flooding waters of the dragon at the conclusion of the 1,260-year prophetic period. This shows that the power represented by the earth beast appears on territory friendly to the church, somewhere after the medieval period. While the first beast arose from the sea, this beast arises from the earth; when mentioned together in Revelation, the earth and the sea represent the whole earth (cf. Revelation 10:2), emphasizing the global scope of Satan's end-time play.

Briefly, this earth beast displays the following characteristics:

- It rises to world power after the sea beast receives the deadly wound—after the French Revolution. This is exclusively an end-time power.
- The second beast is harmless and Christlike in appearance, usurping Christ's symbol of the lamb.
- This lamblike power displays the satanic spirit; it speaks like the dragon, which is a clear reference to the serpent in the Garden of Eden (Genesis 3:1–5).

This end-time earthly power is the true parody of the Holy Spirit. According to the Gospel of John, the purpose of the Holy Spirit is to exercise the authority of Christ, pointing people to Christ (John 15:26; 16:13, 14). In the same way, the earth beast exercises all the authority of the sea beast, pointing people to it (Revelation 13:12).

The "authority of the first beast" (verse 12) refers to the coercive power the medieval church employed during the prophetic period of forty-two months (verses 5–8), imposing doctrines and practices that were contrary to the Bible's teachings. Whoever opposed the teachings of the established church experienced persecution and martyrdom. By exercising this medieval authority, the earth beast will make the people in the world "worship the first beast, whose mortal wound had been healed" (verse 12), counterfeiting the Holy Spirit's role of directing worship to Christ.

How will the earth beast achieve this? As the text shows, the initial phase involves miraculous signs to persuade the people (verses 13, 14; cf. 2 Thessalonians 2:8–10), while the final stage resorts to coercion (Revelation 13:15–17). Just as the Holy Spirit used miraculous signs to convince people to accept Jesus Christ and worship Him, so this counterfeit seeks to deceive people by means of misleading signs and miracles, persuading them to worship the sea beast.

The greatest of the signs performed is bringing fire down from heaven (verse 13). This is reminiscent of the fire Elijah called down from heaven, demonstrating that Yahweh was the one true God of Israel (1 Kings 18:38). The lamblike beast imitates the prophetic role of Elijah and is labeled the false prophet throughout Revelation.

The beast's bringing fire down from heaven also counterfeits the Day of Pentecost, when tongues of fire came down from heaven upon the disciples (Acts 2:3). It follows that bringing fire down from heaven is designed to counterfeit the power of God and to deceive people, convincing them that these miraculous signs are the manifestations of divine power.

The only world power appearing in the postmedieval period and fitting the description of the lamblike beast of Revelation 13 is the Protestant United States. Revelation 13 shows that the United States of America, a historically safe haven for the church, will play a key role in last-day events.

The image of the beast (13:14, 15)

The earth beast will persuade the people of the world to make an image of the sea beast that received the deadly wound. An image is a copy of some reality. This prophecy shows that the world powers will be seduced to create a system of state religion, resembling the one from the Middle Ages. When the civil and political powers join the leading religious organizations to enforce a religion upon people, they will form the image of the beast.

This whole scene mirrors Daniel 3 in which King Nebuchadnezzar orders the people of his kingdom, on threat of death, to worship the golden image he erected. Just as worshiping the golden image was enforced by a legislative decree in Daniel's day, so at the time of the end, the demand for popular worship will be supported by civil power, forcing the whole earth to worship the sea beast.

Revelation 13 indicates that the Protestant United States will assume the leading role in healing the sea beast's deadly wound. It tells us that the religiopolitical system that Satan used during the Middle Ages will rise again in the closing days of this earth's history, winning and controlling the conscience and the worship of the world's people. This prophecy points to the revival of medieval intolerance at the time of the end (Revelation 13:15). The lamblike beast will side with the sea beast to establish a religious union and enforce an institution that characterized medieval Christianity in both western Europe and the Eastern Hemisphere.

The mark of the beast (13:16, 17)

Those who succumb to the pressure applied by this institution will receive a mark with the beast's name on their right hand or their forehead (Revelation 13:16). All classes of human society are commanded to receive the mark of the beast. Receiving this mark means belonging to and worshiping the beast. This mark is the antithesis of God's seal (Revelation 14:1).

While the sealing signifies the Holy Spirit's working presence in human hearts (Ephesians 1:13, 14; 4:30), the mark of the beast counterfeits the work of the Holy Spirit. The people with the mark of the beast have been brought into this religious system and serve it with their hearts and minds; some willingly, others reluctantly.

Placing the mark on the right hand or forehead evokes Deuteronomy 6:8, where Moses instructed the Israelites to bind God's law as a sign upon their hands or their foreheads. This is an injunction Jews have taken literally by wearing phylacteries to show their belonging and obedience to God.[3] This suggests that the mark on the forehead has to do with impressing God's law upon the minds and the behavior of His people. In contrast, receiving the mark of the beast on the right hand or the forehead represents the refusal to obey God's commandments—the exchange of obedience to God for obedience to the beast.

Revelation shows that the first four commandments of the Decalogue—the ones that concern a person's relationship with God and worship—will become the standard of loyalty to God in the final crisis. Satan's end-time activities are portrayed in Revelation as a well-planned attack on these four commandments.

The sea beast's demand for worship (Revelation 13:15) is a direct attack on the first commandment: "You shall have no other gods before Me" (Exodus 20:3, NASB). The earth beast raises up an image of the sea beast to be worshiped (Revelation 13:14, 15), which is a direct attack on the second commandment: "You shall not make for yourself an idol. . . . You shall not worship them or serve them" (Exodus 20:4, 5, NASB). The beast's blasphemy of God (Revelation 13:5, 6) is a direct attack on the third commandment: "You shall not take the name of the LORD your God in vain" (Exodus 20:7, NASB). As explained below, the mark of the beast (Revelation 13:16, 17) is a direct attack on the fourth commandment: "Remember the sabbath day, to keep it holy" (Exodus 20:8, NASB).

Revelation 14:6–12 clearly indicates that the Sabbath commandment, in particular, will be the litmus test of one's faithfulness and obedience to God.[4] The appeal of the three angels' messages to worship and obey the true God rather than to worship the beast and receive the mark of the beast clearly comes in the context of the Sabbath commandment (Revelation 14:7, 9). The Sabbath in the Bible concerns proper worship of and a relationship with God. As the Sabbath is the distinctive sign of God's faithful people's obedience (cf. Exodus 31:12–17; Ezekiel 20:12, 20), so the mark of the beast is the sign of obedience to the beast. The distinctive characteristic of the mark of the beast is the substitution of human commandments for God's commandments. The obvious evidence of this ploy is the human-established false Sabbath—Sunday, the first day of the week—for the seventh-day Sabbath.

Yet observance of Sunday does not in itself mean having the mark of the beast. Sunday keeping will only become "the mark of the beast" when people have a clear understanding of the issues involved in choosing a day of worship.[5] That time is still in the future; but in the present, Christ's followers must not label any individual or group as having the mark of the beast. Sunday keeping today does not render any person lost, just as Sabbath keeping does not make any person a genuine Christian. But the time is soon coming when the mark of the beast will become an issue. It will be a time when every person in the world will choose to take his or her stand for or against God.

1. Ángel Manuel Rodríguez, *Future Glory: The 8 Greatest End-Time Prophecies in the Bible* (Hagerstown, MD: Review and Herald®, 2002), 104.

2. Pope Leo XIII, *Praeclara Gratulationis Publicae* (The Reunion of Christendom), June 20, 1894, quoted in Don F. Neufeld and Julia Neuffer, eds., *Seventh-day Adventist Bible Students' Source Book*, Commentary Reference Series, vol. 9 (Washington, DC: Review and Herald®, 1962), 684.

3. Beatrice S. Neall, "Sealed Saints and the Tribulation," in *Symposium on Revelation—Book 1*, ed. Frank B. Holbrook, Daniel and Revelation Committee Series 6 (Silver Spring, MD: Biblical Research Institute, 1992), 257.

4. William G. Johnsson, "The Saints' End-Time Victory Over the Forces of Evil," in *Symposium on Revelation—Book 2*, ed. Frank B. Holbrook, Daniel and Revelation Committee Series 7 (Silver Spring, MD: Biblical Research Institute, 1992), 30.

5. Richard Rice, *Reign of God*, 2nd ed. (Berrien Springs, MI: Andrews University Press, 1997), 403.

CHAPTER

God's Everlasting Gospel

The previous section, Revelation 12 and 13, provides God's end-time people with firm assurance of Christ's promise to be ever with them during the eschatological showdown. During these hard times, God's people are commissioned to deliver a special message—pictured in terms of three vocal angels flying in midheaven with special messages for the earth's inhabitants.

The Greek word *aggelos* (angel) means "messenger." In the Bible, angels often represent persons in God's service (Malachi 2:7; Luke 1:13). Revelation 14:12 clearly links the three angels to God's end-time people, carrying God's warning message to the world.

The first angel's message (14:6, 7)

The first angel brings the eternal gospel to proclaim to every person on earth. This gospel is good news, and its eternal nature shows that it is the gospel of the Bible. It declares God's message of salvation and judgment. It is good news for those who accept it because they are saved, but it means judgment for those who reject it. The proclamation of the end-time gospel is worldwide, to be proclaimed to "every nation and tribe and tongue and people" (Revelation 14:6). This brings to mind the commission of John to prophesy "concerning many peoples and nations and tongues and kings" (Revelation 10:11). This affirms the notion that the three angels represent God's end-time people, who are entrusted with the preaching of the gospel. This preaching is significant because the beast, at the time of the end, will exercise its Satan-delegated authority over "every tribe and people and tongue and nation" (Revelation 13:7). Just as Satan's deceptive activities are worldwide, so also is the end-time proclamation of the gospel. This preaching of the gospel is referenced by Jesus in His sermon on the Mount of Olives (Matthew 24:14).

The angel proclaims the message with "a loud voice" (Revelation 14:7; Greek *phōnē megalē*, from which the word *megaphone* comes). This message is urgent; it concerns the eternal destiny of every person on earth. It is God's call to repentance. This call is expressed with a triple imperative: to fear God, to give Him glory, and to worship Him as the Creator.

"Fear God, and give Him glory" (Revelation 14:7). In Revelation, God's end-time people are the ones who fear God (Revelation 11:18; 19:5). To fear God in the Bible means to take Him seriously and acknowledge Him for who He is. It implies respect and reverence for God. Fearing God denotes a right relationship with Him and a full surrender to His will (Genesis 22:12; Job 1:8, 9). It results in rightdoing, and those who fear God keep His commandments (Deuteronomy 5:29; 13:4; Ecclesiastes 12:13).

Fearing God and giving Him glory go together (Revelation 11:13; 15:4). While the former designates a right relationship with God, the latter denotes obedience to Him. The person who fears God responds to His grace by keeping His commandments. Jesus states, "My Father is glorified by this, that you bear much fruit" (John 15:8, NASB). God's end-time people are characterized by their close relationship with Jesus Christ and by keeping His commandments (Revelation 12:17; 14:12).

The reason for fearing God and giving Him glory is because "the hour of His judgment has come" (Revelation 14:7). This judgment is the pre-Advent judgment that takes place prior to the Second Coming; this is in contrast to the final judgment that takes place after the millennium (Revelation 20:11–15). Its purpose is to decide who is in a right relationship with God and who is not. Those decisions are made before Jesus comes. This pre-Advent judgment takes place at the same time as the end-time gospel is preached. When the preaching of the gospel is completed and the pre-Advent judgment is concluded, there will be a final separation between those who are for the kingdom and those who are lost (Revelation 14:14–20). Then Jesus will come to bring His reward to every person, according to his or her deeds.

Judgment is a part of the gospel. It is good news for the faithful and obedient but bad news for the unfaithful. When the judgment is finished, the destiny of every person is decided (Revelation 22:11). There will be no second chance. The offer of salvation will no longer be available. To God's people, judgment means vindication and salvation; but to others, it brings condemnation. It is to the latter that the messages of the three angels are directed, calling them to worship the Living God. Sinners still have an opportunity to repent and turn to God because He does not want anyone to perish. Rather, He wants "all to come to repentance" (2 Peter 3:9, NASB).

"Worship Him who made the heaven and the earth and sea and springs of waters" (Revelation 14:7). Worship is central in the final conflict between Christ and Satan. At the time of the end, people in the world will fall into two groups: those who fear and worship God, and those who fear and worship the beast. A clear line is drawn between the two groups. It is important to keep in mind that the end-time test is not a denial of worship but a denial of *who* is worshiped. While most of the world's people reject the truth and choose to follow and worship the beast, God's people choose to worship and serve God.

True worship in the Bible is associated with a correct day for worship. The call to worship God who made the heaven and the earth and the sea and the springs of waters reflects the fourth of the Ten Commandments. The editors of *The Greek New Testament* note in a margin that this statement from

Revelation 14:7 is a direct quotation from Exodus 20:11.[1] This indicates that the first angel's call to worship God the Creator is given in the context of Sabbath observance. This is a call to worship God, who created this earth in six days and proclaimed the seventh day holy (Genesis 2:1–3). The seventh-day Sabbath is a special sign of our relationship with God (Exodus 31:13; Ezekiel 20:12, 20). It is a memorial of both Creation (Exodus 20:11) and redemption (Deuteronomy 5:15).

The first angel's message shows that the truth about God the Creator will once more be proclaimed to the world. People will be called to return to God, countering Satan's deceptive activities, which are intended to pull the world into false religion and service to a counterfeit god (2 Thessalonians 2:4).

The second angel's message (14:8)

The second angel's message is closely related to the first message. While the first one calls the people to fear and worship God the Creator, the second message announces the fall of Babylon the great—the counterfeit god—"who has made all the nations drink the wine of the passion of her immorality" (Revelation 14:8).

The symbol of Babylon in Revelation is rooted in historical Babylon as the power that opposed God and oppressed His people. From its inception at the Tower of Babel, Babylon has been characterized by arrogance and rebellion against God (Genesis 11:1–9). Isaiah 14:4, 12–15 equates Babylon with Satan and his attempt to make himself equal to God. In Revelation 14:8, the expression "Babylon the great" echoes the boasting of King Nebuchadnezzar (Daniel 4:30). This boasting was met with the announcement of divine judgment on him, and Babylon would not be the eternal kingdom Nebuchadnezzar envisioned.

The end-time Babylon in Revelation is symbolic of the satanic trinity—Satan, the sea beast, and the earth beast. This satanic league will unite apostate religious powers under its auspices; these are referred to as Babylon's daughters (Revelation 17:5). They will put themselves into the service of Satan in opposition to God and His people (Revelation 13:11–18). This apostate religious confederacy is characterized by the pride and arrogance of historical Babylon. Like Babylon of old, it exalts itself above God, seeking to take God's place. Revelation 17 pictures end-time Babylon as a prostitute making all nations drink her wine and seducing them into illicit relationships with her (Revelation 17:1–5; 18:3). Jeremiah speaks of Babylon "intoxicating all the earth. The nations have drunk of her wine; therefore the nations are going mad" (Jeremiah 51:7, NASB). In Revelation 13:11–18, the satanic trinity deceives and seduces the people in the world to worship the beast and its image. The seduced nations will associate with end-time Babylon for economic security (Revelation 18:3, 9–19). The medieval system of state religion will be restored, and the mortal wound of the beast will be healed. The newly established religiopolitical union will enforce false religion, controlling people's consciences and conduct. The world's people will be coerced into worship of the beast and acceptance of its mark.

The second angel's message provides an assurance to God's people that this wicked system will not last long. It is already fallen and will soon come to its end, just like Babylon of old (cf. Isaiah 21:9; Jeremiah 51:8). In Revelation 14:8, the twofold repetition of the word *fallen* points out that Babylon will certainly end. This collapse is portrayed in Revelation 18.

The third angel's message (14:9-11)
The third angel follows, and his message builds on the previous two. While the other two messages call people to true worship and announce the doom of Babylon, the message of the third angel delivers a serious warning to those who choose to worship the beast and its image and receive the mark on their foreheads or on their right hands.

This angel uses drastic language. All who choose to drink of Babylon's wine will have to "drink of the wine of the wrath of God, which is mixed in full strength in the cup of His anger" (Revelation 14:10). In the Old Testament, drinking wine from the Lord's cup is a frequent symbol of God's wrath (Job 21:20;

Psalm 75:8; Isaiah 51:17–23). In ancient times, wine was often diluted with water to reduce its strength. Undiluted wine was mixed with various herbs and spices to increase its intoxicating strength. The mixed, undiluted wine represents God's wrath being fully executed without mercy. The psalmist applies this metaphor to divine judgment: "For a cup is in the hand of the Lord, and the wine foams; it is well mixed, and He pours out of this" (Psalm 75:8, NASB).

Drinking this undiluted cup of God's wrathful wine is portrayed in Revelation 15 and 16 as the seven last plagues. The seven last plagues are spoken of as the cup of the wine of God's fierce wrath, poured out on those who worship the beast and receive the mark of the beast (Revelation 16:1, 19). In pouring out the seven last plagues, "the wrath of God is completed" (Revelation 15:1).

All who worship the beast's image and receive the mark of the beast will be tormented with eternal fire before the angels and the Lamb. The smoke of the fire is described as ascending forever and ever, giving people no rest day or night. This is a well-known image in the Bible. Fire and sulfur in the Old Testament are symbols of judgment (Genesis 19:24; Isaiah 34:8–10). The concept of eternal fire and smoke ascending forever also comes from the Old Testament. Isaiah prophesied that Edom would be destroyed by fire and sulfur and become a burning pitch: "It will not be quenched night or day; its smoke will go up forever," and it will never rise again from its ruins (Isaiah 34:10, NASB). Jude described the fate of Sodom and Gomorrah as suffering "the punishment of eternal fire" (Jude 7, NASB). It seems clear that these texts do not talk about endless burning. Neither Sodom and Gomorrah nor Edom are burning in modern Jordan. But the effects of the fire that destroyed them last forever. The same is true regarding the eternal fire in Revelation; it does not denote endless burning but burning long enough to make consumption complete— until nothing is left to burn.

The Old Testament prophets used the destruction of Sodom and Gomorrah as the model for destroying ancient Babylon

(Isaiah 13:19; Jeremiah 50:40). The same language is employed in Revelation 14 to describe the fate of end-time Babylon. The grotesque and fearful language points to total annihilation and not to an eternal burning and suffering. Those who choose to worship the beast and its image and acquire the mark of the beast will receive eternal punishment, thus sharing the fate of Babylon the great (Revelation 19:3; 20:10).

The vivid language used in the third angel's message is intended to stir up people's senses and move them to stand firm in the face of Satan's end-time deception. Fear is expelled by a greater fear. As the earth beast of Revelation 13 uses fear to compel the world's people to choose false religion and receive the mark of the beast, Revelation uses even stronger language to dispel that fear, echoing the words of Jesus, "Do not fear those who kill the body but are unable to kill the soul; but rather fear Him who is able to destroy both soul and body in hell" (Matthew 10:28, NASB). Those who respond to the call and choose God can escape the fate of the satanic trinity and their followers (Revelation 20:11–15).

The end-time saints (14:12, 13)

The three angels' messages conclude with a positive statement. They point to the saints' endurance. These saints are entrusted with preaching the end-time gospel message (Revelation 14:12) and are the same people spoken of in Revelation 12:17, who are the objects of Satan's furious rage and attack. They are characterized by their unswerving faithfulness to Christ and their obedience to God's commandments. In Revelation 14:12, the word *here* in the phrase "here is the perseverance of the saints" shows that their endurance is primarily because of their faithful preaching of the end-time gospel.

These saints are promised rest if they suffer physical hardship and persecution, even to the point of death (cf. Revelation 12:11). This rest from their labors, along with their good works, will follow them. This promise contrasts with the threat to those who worship the beast and receive its mark; they will never have rest (Revelation 14:11). The eternal destiny of God's people is secured by Christ, who promised to always be with them, until the very end of the age (see Matthew 28:20).

Revelation uses vivid language to warn those who read the book about the serious nature of their choices. Heeding the call to "fear God, and give Him glory" (Revelation 14:7, NASB) is the only way to escape the fate of the satanic trinity.

---

1. See Kurt Aland et al., eds., *The Greek New Testament*, 4th ed. (New York: United Bible Societies, 1993), 863.

The Seven Last Plagues

Revelation 15 and 16 build on the vision of the two harvests in Revelation 14:14–20. This vision pictures the saints as wheat to be gathered into Christ's barn (Revelation 14:14–16; cf. Matthew 13:30, 31) and the unrepentant as grapes to be trodden in the winepress of His wrath (Revelation 14:17–20).

Timing of the plagues

Revelation 16:1–11 tells us that the seven last plagues are reserved exclusively for those who reject God and receive the mark of the beast. They are specified as "the last" (Revelation 15:1) because they follow the seven trumpet plagues (Revelation 8; 9; 11:15–19). The trumpets were preliminary judgments, anticipating more severe judgment plagues yet to come. Although there are similarities in the language between the trumpet plagues and the last plagues, the two series are not the same.

First, during the trumpets, the gospel is preached throughout the world (Revelation 10:8; 11–14) and the mediatory ministry of Christ goes on in heaven (Revelation 8:3–5). But the last plagues are clearly poured out after the preaching of the gospel is finished and the intercession in the heavenly sanctuary is concluded (Revelation 14:6–13).

Second, Revelation 15:8 illustrates that the temple in heaven became "filled with smoke from the glory of God and from His power; and no one was able to enter the temple." This language is derived from both the dedication of the tabernacle in the wilderness during Israel's exodus (Exodus 40:34, 35) and from Solomon's temple (1 Kings 8:10, 11). On both occasions, the cloud of God's glory filled the building, so the priests could not enter to minister before God. With the absence of the priests, there was no intercession in the temple. Revelation 15:8 reflects this idea, telling us that before the seven plagues are poured out on rebellious humanity, Christ's mediatory ministry in heaven will be concluded. The door of opportunity will ultimately close, and the destiny of every person will be decided (Revelation 14:14–20).

Third, the trumpet plagues are restricted in scope and effect. They affect only a part of Satan's kingdom—the phrase "a third" is constantly repeated in the text (Revelation 8:7–12; 9:15, 18). No restriction is linked to the seven plagues. They are evidently more extensive. Note the statement that "every living thing in the sea died" (Revelation 16:3).

Last, the seven trumpets cover a long span of history, from the first century until the Second Coming. Relatively long time periods are linked to them (Revelation 9:5, 15; 11:2, 11), whereas no prophetic time frame is specified for the seven last plagues. They affect humanity at the end of history for a relatively short period of time prior to the Second Coming and occur within the seventh-trumpet time frame.

The purpose of the plagues

The plagues are redemptive in nature. Just as God sent the plagues on Egypt to deliver His people and take them to the Promised Land (Exodus 7–12), here God sends the seven last plagues to defeat His enemies and deliver His people from those who want to destroy them.

Second, the last plagues are punitive (Revelation 15:1; 16:2). In Revelation 6:9–11, the martyred saints are pictured as crying to God for vindication. Their cry is representative of all

God's suffering people throughout history. Now, with the outpouring of the seven last plagues, their prayers are ultimately answered and God's people are vindicated.

Third, the seven last plagues are intended to bring rebellious humanity to the realization of the consequences of their choices and actions. In Revelation 13, the people of the world have chosen to follow Babylon. As God withdraws His protection from the world, the seven last plagues are poured out on the earth with devastating effect. Now people are forced to consider the consequences of their choices. Yet their continual resistance to God's merciful call has left them unrepentant.

Like the Egyptian plagues, the seven last plagues are intended to disclose the hardness of the hearts of those who rejected the gospel (cf. Exodus 7:1–5). As severe as the last plagues are, they do not move people to repentance. Just as each of the Egyptian plagues increased the hardness of the hearts of Pharaoh and his officials, so each plague coming upon the worshipers of the satanic trinity hardens their hearts into an even greater hatred of God and His people (Revelation 16:9–11).

Literal or symbolic?

An important and difficult question concerns the nature of the plagues. Are they literal or symbolic? Revelation's language is often symbolic, which seems obvious when interpreting the seals and the trumpets. But the situation seems different with the seven last plagues. The fact that the first five plagues inflict intense physical pain and suffering, causing people to curse God, shows that they are literal (verses 8–11). This is affirmed in Revelation 7:16; this verse states that the 144,000 will not hunger or thirst anymore and neither the scorching sun nor the heat will again affect them. These seem to be literal trials.

But the sixth plague, leading to the battle of Armageddon, contains symbolic and spiritual language. And the final plague, addressing the fall of end-time Babylon, seems to blend literal and symbolic meaning.

In all of this, it is important to remember that the seven last plagues are a prophecy yet to be fulfilled. The true nature of the prophecy will be fully understood when it is fulfilled. Whether literal or figurative, the seven last plagues will expose the impotence of the satanic trinity to help suffering humanity and will vindicate God and His government.

The first five plagues (16:1-11)

A voice from the temple in heaven—the place where intercession was previously taking place—commands the seven angels to pour out the plagues on those who have sided with the satanic trinity and received the mark of the beast (Revelation 16:1). The time has come for God to vindicate His faithful people and bring His righteous judgments upon those who harmed them.

The first angel pours his bowl on the earth, and painful sores strike those who have the mark of the beast. This disease is described as painful and incurable, covering the entire body (cf. Deuteronomy 28:35; Job 2:7). A plague of this kind struck the Egyptians during the Exodus (Exodus 9:10, 11). The victims of this plague are those who have the mark of the beast and worship the beast's image. The first plague carries out the threat of the third angel's message: those who have the mark and worship the beast and its image must now drink undiluted wine from the cup of God's wrath (Revelation 14:9, 10).

The second angel pours his bowl into the sea, and the sea becomes like the blood of a dead man. Every living thing in it dies.

The third angel pours his bowl into the rivers and the springs of water. Immediately, the water on the earth turns into blood; and without water to drink, rebellious humanity has no chance of survival.

The fourth angel pours his bowl on the sun, and intense heat scorches people, causing unbearable pain. The pain, however, does not move them to repentance because they have hardened their hearts to such an extent that they cannot repent. Instead, they curse and blaspheme the name of God, railing against Him whom they have rejected and following in the footsteps of the blasphemous beast (Revelation 13:6).

While the first four plagues affect the general population, the fifth plague strikes the beast's throne, bringing total darkness over the earth. This scene mirrors Egypt's ninth plague of intense darkness, which covered the entire land of the rebellious nation (Exodus 10:21–23).

It is important to remember that Satan delegates the throne and authority to the sea beast of Revelation 13 (Revelation 13:2). With the support of the earth beast, the sea beast begins to exercise its authority over the earth, deceiving and then coercing the world's people to side with the satanic trinity. Yet even this overwhelming power, the seat of Satan's authority, cannot withstand the force of these plagues.

The power of the sea beast is now undermined as it suffers humiliation before the people. As earth's inhabitants gnaw their tongues in pain, they become enraged, realizing the impotence of the unholy trinity's abilities to protect them from the effects of the plagues. They feel deceived. Yet, as in the case of Egypt's pharaoh, the terror and pain of the plagues increasingly hardens their hearts. They have set their minds against God. They continue to curse and blaspheme Him for their pain and sores and refuse to repent (Revelation 16:11). They are being readied for the final deception; when they turn their anger against God's people, Satan draws them into the great battle between God and Satan. The nefarious scheme is in place and plays out in the sixth plague (verses 12–16).

The drying up of the Euphrates (16:12a)

The imagery of the drying of the Euphrates is rooted in the fall of historical Babylon. In 539 B.C., Persia's Cyrus the Great came with his armies and besieged the city. Because of Babylon's strong fortifications and abundant supply of water and food, the people felt their city was impregnable. But on the night the leaders were partying in King Belshazzar's palace, the city was captured by the Persian army (Daniel 5). Ancient historians note that the Persians diverted the Euphrates River and entered the city through the dried riverbed, taking it by surprise.[1] Because of Babylon's overthrow, God's people were allowed to return to their homeland.

The capture of ancient Babylon by Cyrus is the background for the sixth plague scene. As in the case of ancient Babylon, here the symbolic drying up of the Euphrates River results in the collapse of end-time Babylon. This scene must be understood symbolically, because as stated earlier, the Euphrates in Revelation represents the world's civil, secular, and political powers, giving their support to Babylon (Revelation 17:15). Those powers will eventually withdraw their support from Babylon and turn against it (verses 15–17), drying up the Euphrates River.

Up to the fifth plague, the world's people have focused their hope on Babylon for protection. As they experience upheavals in nature, they hope Babylon will protect them. But as the fifth plague strikes the very seat of the beast's authority, the disillusioned people realize the impotence of Babylon to protect them from the plagues' effects (Revelation 16:10). Feeling deceived and filled with hostility, they unite against Babylon and destroy it (Revelation 17:16, 17).

The three froglike demons (16:13, 14)

The drying of the Euphrates River shakes the satanic trinity— the dragon, the sea beast, and the earth beast, which is referred to as the false prophet. At this point, Satan and his two associates gather the whole world for the final deception. Proceeding from the mouths of the satanic trinity are three froglike, demonic spirits going out to the leaders of the world "to gather them together for the war of the great day of God, the Almighty" (Revelation 16:14). These demons are the very "breath" of the satanic trinity in the last deception.

The froglike spirits are reminiscent of the frog plague in Egypt (Exodus 8:1–15). It was the last plague of Moses that Pharaoh's magicians were able to duplicate and use their twisted influence to push Pharaoh to his persistent opposition of God; ultimately Pharaoh rejected God's message through Moses. In light of this Old Testament background, the three froglike demons of the sixth plague are Satan's last attempt to counterfeit God's work. They are portrayed as the counterpart to the three angels in Revelation 14, sent out with a false gospel to persuade the world's secular and political authorities to side with them against God and His people in preparation for the great day of God Almighty.

Thus, these froglike demons are Satan's powerful agents, who will entice the earth's people into the final battle. This situation recalls the "deceiving spirit" (1 Kings 22:22) that enticed King Ahab to refuse the message sent to him from God and choose the battlefront (verses 21–23). Satan is determined to be victorious in the final crisis and enables the demonic spirits to perform miraculous signs. Their method of persuasion is deception, which fits perfectly with Satan's end-time plan to draw people to his side rather than God's (Revelation 13:13, 14).

The activities of the demonic trinity result in great success. The nations of the world are again deceived and submit their powers to Satan. They are fully arrayed against God's people, and the stage is set for the final battle.

Gathering for Armageddon (16:16)

The world powers will gather at the place that in Hebrew is called *Armageddon*, meaning "the mountain of Megiddo." In the Old Testament, Megiddo was a fortress-city, located in the Plain of Esdraelon at the foot of the Carmel mountain range. The city stood on the crucial choke point along the great highway from Egypt to Damascus, making it a key strategic site. Unsurprisingly, the region was known for several famous battles (cf. Judges 5:19–21; 6:33; 1 Samuel 31; 2 Kings 9:27; 23:29, 30).

Specifically, the mount of Megiddo is associated with Mount Carmel, which is the site of the battle between Elijah and the prophets of Baal over who was the true God—the Lord or Baal (1 Kings 18:21). The fire that fell from heaven to the earth demonstrated that the Lord was the only true God (verses 38, 39). In the final battle, however, the earth beast brings fire down from heaven to counterfeit God's work and to deceive the whole world (Revelation 13:13, 14).

Armageddon will finally resolve the great controversy—namely, who is the legitimate ruler of the universe. It is not a military battle fought in the Middle East. Rather, it is a spiritual battle between Christ and His followers and the forces of darkness. It is a battle for the minds of the people (2 Corinthians 10:4, 5). Its outcome will be like that of the Carmel conflict—God's ultimate triumph over the forces of darkness.

Revelation 16:12–16 does not portray the actual battle but only the great gathering of the religious and political powers to Armageddon. The actual battle follows the sixth plague and is described in Revelation 16:17–19:21. John later sees "the beast and the kings of the earth and their armies gathered to make war" against Christ, who is coming from heaven while accompanied by His army of the saints (Revelation 19:19; cf. Revelation 17:14). The battle will conclude with the defeat of the beast and his armies (Revelation 19:20, 21) by the legitimate King of kings and Lord of lords (verse 16).

---

1. Herodotus, *The Histories* 1.191. Herodotus's description of Babylon's capture by Cyrus has been confirmed in modern times by the Cyrus Cylinder, which describes the capture of Babylon by the Persians without any battle. See James B. Pritchard, *Ancient Near Eastern Texts Relating to the Old Testament*, 3rd ed. (Princeton, NJ: Princeton University Press, 1969), 315.

Judgment on Babylon

Babylon dwells on many waters (17:1b, 2)

One of the seven angels with the bowls of God's wrath invites John to witness the judgment of Babylon, "the great prostitute" (Revelation 17:1). The angel states that the prostitute Babylon "dwells on many waters" (verse 1b). Jeremiah 51:13 shows that "many waters" refers to the Euphrates River. The angel later explains to John that these waters symbolize civil, secular, and political world powers (Revelation 17:15). That Babylon—the end-time union of religious authorities—is pictured as sitting on the worldwide powers illustrates that, at the time of the end, these two entities are distinct; something that was not the case in the past. Throughout history and particularly the Middle Ages, the political powers and the established religious authority went hand in hand. Nations were governed by religiopolitical powers. Revelation 13:1–10 portrays the medieval church, led by the papacy, as a religiopolitical power dominating the Western world during the prophetic 1,260-day period. But at the time of the end, these two entities will remain distinct, yet will work together for a common purpose.

Just as ancient Babylon depended on the Euphrates River for its existence, so end-time Babylon will depend on the civil, secular, and political world powers to enforce its plans and purposes. This end-time religious confederacy will form an alliance with the governing world powers. These powers will place themselves in the service of this apostate religious system, working against Christ and His faithful people during the end-time crisis.

Two groups are specified as being seduced by Babylon in the final crisis. The first are "the kings of the earth," portrayed as committing adultery with the prostitute Babylon (Revelation 17:2). These are the governing political world powers. In the Old Testament, the language of fornication is frequently used to describe Israel aligning itself with pagan nations (Isaiah 1:21; Jeremiah 3:1–10; Ezekiel 16; 23). The adulterous relationship between "the kings of the earth" and the prostitute Babylon symbolizes an illicit union between the end-time religious confederacy and the world's governing political leaders in the final crisis (Revelation 17:2).

The second group mentioned are "those who dwell on the earth," who are spiritually drunk with the wine of Babylon's immorality (Revelation 17:2, 8; cf. Revelation 14:8). This is the general populace—not the world's leaders. While the world's leaders commit adultery with the prostitute Babylon, the rest of earth's people are intoxicated by her deceptive teachings and activities, enticing them to worship the beast (Revelation 14:8; 18:3). When people are drunk, they do not think soberly and realize too late the nature of their bad decisions and actions.

Both groups are equally deceived and have put themselves under the control of Babylon for political and economic benefit. Revelation tells us that the world will once again be united at the time of the end and religion will dominate in the way it did during the Middle Ages. The time will come when the world's people will realize their bad choices and turn against Babylon; but just the same, it will be too late.

The prostitute riding the beast (17:3-6)

John was told that the prostitute Babylon sat on many waters. Now he is carried in vision to the wilderness, where he sees a woman sitting on a scarlet beast (Revelation 17:3). While the prostitute represents the end-time union of religion, the beast symbolizes the worldwide confederacy of political powers. The prophecy states that, at the end of time, the political powers on earth will join the service of end-time Babylon. Babylon, the woman sitting on the beast, will use her religious system to dominate the political powers during the end-time crisis.

She is pictured as extravagantly dressed in purple and scarlet, lavishly adorned with ornaments of gold and precious stones. On her forehead is the inscription "Babylon the great, the mother of harlots" (verse 5). The scarlet color of the woman's dress corresponds to the scarlet color of the beast she sits upon (verses 3, 4). Scarlet is also the color of blood and oppression, which conforms with the character of this religious system that is "drunk with the blood of the saints and with the blood of the witnesses of Jesus" (verse 6). Purple is used for royal attire (Judges 8:26; Esther 8:15; Daniel 5:7) and fits the prostitute's quest for control of the world.

The woman's dress evokes the attire of the high priest in the Old Testament, which included purple, scarlet, and gold (Exodus 28:5, 6). Her forehead inscription resembles the inscription "Holy to the LORD" on the miter of the high priest (verses 36, NASB). Also, the cup in her hand reflects the drink offering in the sanctuary (Exodus 30:9; Leviticus 23:13). Her description is strikingly similar to the New Jerusalem (Revelation 21). All this suggests that the Babylon of Revelation 17 refers to an end-time religious system rather than a political power. With its historic Christian appearance, this end-time religious system becomes Satan's powerful tool to deceive and seduce the world into apostasy during the final crisis.

Although she appears in religious garb, Babylon is a prostitute and the mother of prostitutes, seducing the world away from God. She is drunk with the blood of the saints who died because of their witness to Jesus Christ (cf. Revelation 6:9). This religious system, which makes all people drunk with its false teachings, is itself drunk with the blood of Christ's followers. This clearly links end-time Babylon with the beast of Revelation 13, which represents medieval apostate Christianity in western Europe that was led by the papacy and responsible for the deaths of millions of Christians who were persecuted for their faithful witness to the gospel. The time is coming, however, when God will judge this "great prostitute" and avenge "the blood of His servants from her hand" (Revelation 17:1; 19:2).

John is astonished at this prostitute, and his reaction denotes his recognition of her. He sees her in the desert (Revelation 17:3) and recognizes her as the woman who fled into the wilderness to escape the persecution of the dragon during the 1,260-day prophetic period of the Middle Ages (Revelation 12:13, 14). This suggests that this end-time opponent of God's people was once Christ's faithful church. This explains why, at the time of the end, Satan is filled with great animosity toward the remnant of the woman's offspring rather than at the woman (verse 17). At the time of the end, the church that in times past was faithful to God will turn into an enemy of God's faithful remnant—those who keep His commandments and have the testimony of Jesus.

The resurrected beast (17:6-8)

As previously established, the prostitute Babylon symbolizes the end-time union of religious authorities, and the beast symbolizes a worldwide political union. These two are inseparable, for the prostitute derives her character and power from the beast. As the medieval church used political power to control the minds and beliefs of people, so Babylon will use the world's governing political powers at the time of the end.

The scarlet beast is identified as the one that "was, and is not, and is about to come up out of the abyss" (Revelation 17:8). The phrase "was, and is not, and is about to come up" is, first, a parody of the divine name Yahweh—"who was and who is and who is coming"—in Revelation 4:8 (cf. Revelation 1:4, 8). Second, this tripartite formula further shows that the beast has passed through three phases of its existence: past, present, and future.

First, the beast "was"; it existed in the past. There are clear links between this scarlet beast and the sea beast of Revelation 13 that recovered from its deadly wound. Both beasts are full of blasphemous names and have seven heads and ten horns (Revelation 17:3, 7). This shows that the "was" phase of the beast refers to its activities during the prophetic period of 1,260 days (cf. Revelation 13:5). Then, with its deadly wound, the beast came into its "is not" phase (verse 3). In other words, it disappeared for some time, yet it survived.

The beast will come to life again in full satanic rage against God's faithful people during the end time (Revelation 12:17). The resurrection of the beast will prompt the admiration of "those who dwell on the earth, whose names have not been written in the book of life from the foundation of the world" (Revelation 17:8b).

This beast of Revelation 17 is the sea beast of Revelation 13, after the healing of its deadly wound. It is upon this resurrected beast that the end-time prostitute Babylon sits. This end-time religious system is a continuation of the religiopolitical power that oppressed God's people during the 1,260-day prophetic period. Revelation makes it clear that religion will once again dominate and control politics as it did during the Middle Ages. But there is a noticeable difference between the medieval period and the time of the end. While the sea beast, representing the medieval church, was a religiopolitical power, the scarlet beast is exclusively a political power. Religious and political powers are distinct at the end of time.

The seven heads of the beast (17:9-11)

At this point, the angel makes a call for wisdom. The wisdom here is the same spoken of in connection with 666 as the number of the beast (Revelation 13:18). This wisdom refers to spiritual discernment rather than brilliant mental and intellectual ability—such discernment is only imparted by the Spirit (James 1:5). Only through this divinely imparted wisdom will God's end-time people be able to recognize the true character of this satanic power.

The angel explains that the existence and activities of the

beast are identified with its heads. Throughout history, the beast has ruled and been active through its heads. The angel explains to John that these seven heads are "seven mountains" that actually symbolize "seven kings" (Revelation 17:9, 10). The waters, the mountains, the beast, and the kings are symbols used to describe the political powers that provide support for end-time Babylon in its work of persecuting God's people.

Mountains often represent world powers or empires (Jeremiah 51:25; Daniel 2:35). Thus, the seven mountains upon which Babylon sits, stand for seven successive empires that have dominated the world throughout history and through which Satan has worked to oppose God.[1] Sharing the common traits of religiopolitical governance and coercion, these empires have persecuted and destroyed God's people.

The angel further explains to John that five of these world empires have fallen, one is, and the seventh one was not yet active during the time of John. Remember that the angel explains the meaning of these kingdoms to John from his own temporal perspective, not ours. In such a way, the "one is" kingdom is the Roman Empire of John's time. The five that have fallen are thus the empires that ruled the world and harmed God's people prior to John's time:

- Egypt was the world power that enslaved and oppressed Israel, seeking to destroy it.
- Assyria destroyed and scattered the ten tribes of Israel.
- Babylon destroyed Jerusalem and took Judah into exile.
- Persia almost annihilated the Jews at the time of Esther.
- Greece oppressed and tried to destroy the Jews through Antiochus IV Epiphanes.

The seventh kingdom that "has not yet come" was still a future manifestation from John's perspective, arising after the fall of the Roman Empire. The best interpretation is that the seventh head is the sea beast of Revelation 13, which represents the medieval church, headed by the papacy.

The seventh kingdom is said to remain for a short time

(Revelation 17:10). In this instance, the Greek adjectival word for "a short time" is *oligon*, meaning "short" or "little." It is different from *mikron*, which is used in Revelation to indicate "a shortness of time" (see Revelation 6:11; 20:3). In contrast, *oligon* does not indicate a length of time; rather, it is used in a qualitative sense. For example, Revelation 12:12 states that after being cast out of heaven, Satan realized that "he has little time." This "little time" does not indicate a length of time, for it has been thousands of years since his expulsion from heaven. Rather, it indicates that Satan realized that his time was limited.

That the seventh kingdom must remain for a short time does not point to the length of its existence; rather, the doom of this kingdom is determined by God ("it must remain"; Revelation 17:10), and it will come to its end. The deadly wound it received took place during the French Revolution in 1798.

This seventh head will reappear as the eighth head and exercise political power the way it did during the Middle Ages. It is through this eighth head that the scarlet beast works. We live in the era of the seventh head, and the eighth head with its ten united kingdoms has no power as of yet. It will appear on the worldwide scene during the time of the end and impose its apostate religious system on the earth's inhabitants.

The ten horns of the beast (17:12, 13)

The angel explains that the ten horns of the scarlet beast represent the ten kings who will receive dominion with the beast during the time of the eighth head. The book does not explain exactly who these ten kings are. Because this passage is about a prophecy that is yet to be fulfilled, only the future will fully reveal the identity of these end-time powers.

All that can be learned from the text is that the ten kings (meaning kingdoms) compose a powerful confederacy of the world's nations. They are end-time powers. Their number denotes the totality of the world's nations, joining themselves under the control of the satanic trinity. They are evidently the governing political powers spoken of in Revelation 17:2, who are involved in the adulterous relationship with Babylon. These world powers will render their allegiance to the beast; something that will last for only a short time—one hour in prophetic terms. The beast will use them to enforce its plans and purposes.

The battle of Armageddon (17:14-18)

At this point, Revelation once again briefly describes the battle of Armageddon—introduced in Revelation 16:12–16 and concluded in Revelation 19:11–21. Induced by Babylon, the worldwide political powers will engage in war with the Lamb (Revelation 17:14). This shows that the final battle is not a military conflict in the Middle East between Jews and various Muslim nations. Rather, it is a spiritual clash between Satan's confederacy and Christ with His faithful people. Babylon's aim is to defeat Christ and destroy His people, but Christ will triumph over this end-time religiopolitical confederacy.

Dramatically, the ten horns and the beast (the political powers) suddenly turn against the prostitute Babylon (the false religious system). The political and secular powers that enabled Babylon to dominate the world withdraw their support and, enraged, turn against her. This withdrawal of support from Babylon is pictured in the sixth plague as the Euphrates River drying up (Revelation 16:12). As Revelation 16 indicates, the deceived political powers have become disillusioned because of Babylon's impotence to protect them from the plagues (verses 10, 11). They feel deceived and, filled with antagonism and hostility, attack and ruin her.

John again employs Old Testament language used for the judgments that fell upon adulterous Jerusalem (Jeremiah 4:30; Ezekiel 16:35–41; 23:22–29). The furious and disillusioned political powers will make the prostitute Babylon "desolate and naked and will eat her flesh and will burn her up with fire" (Revelation 17:16). Burning by fire was the punishment for a high priest's daughter who was involved in prostitution (Leviticus 21:9), which is another indication that the prostitute Babylon denotes a religious system that was once true to God but, at the time of the end, will turn away from Him and become unfaithful.

The scene concludes with a reminder that God is in control and that the wicked may go no further than God allows them (Revelation 17:17). The actions of the deceived political powers carry out God's judgment upon Babylon and ultimately conclude God's purposes in the end-time crisis.

Revelation 18 continues the theme of the destruction of Babylon from the previous chapter. This apostate religious system has filled her cup of abomination and is about to receive the cup of the wine of God's wrath (Revelation 16:19). In chapter 17, the judgment on this end-time apostate religious system is pictured in terms of the prostitute's execution (according to the Mosaic Law); and in chapter 18, it is portrayed as a wealthy commercial city sinking into the sea.

---

1. William G. Johnsson, "The Saints' End-Time Victory Over the Forces of Evil," in *Symposium on Revelation—Book 2*, ed. Frank B. Holbrook, Daniel and Revelation Committee Series 7 (Silver Spring, MD: Biblical Research Institute, 1992), 17.

"I Make All Things New"

Finally, we come to the end, or rather, the new beginning of the world as it was meant to be. The conclusion of Revelation is the culmination of world history.

Wedding supper of the Lamb

In Revelation 19, the wedding supper scene reflects ancient Jewish wedding practices. The prospective groom would go to the house of the bride-to-be's father for the betrothal. After the groom paid the dowry, the groom and the bride were considered legally married, although they could not yet live together. The groom would then return to his father's house to prepare the place where he and his bride would live. The bride stayed at her father's house to prepare herself for the wedding. When the preparations were complete, the groom would come back to the bride's father's house, and the wedding feast would take place. Afterward, he would take his bride to the place he had prepared, and they would live together.

In a similar manner, Christ left His Father's house in heaven to come to the earth to betroth His bride—the church. After paying the dowry with His life at Calvary, He returned to His Father's house to prepare a place for His bride. He promised to come back and take His bride to Himself (John 14:2, 3). His bride remained on the earth, preparing herself. At the end of history, Christ will come back, and the long-awaited wedding will take place. He will finally be united with His bride, the church, and take her to His Father's house.

During this period, His people prepare themselves for that long-anticipated event. According to Paul, when Christ comes, He desires to see His church without "spot or wrinkle or any such thing; but that she would be holy and blameless" (Ephesians 5:27, NASB). Here, in Revelation 19:7, 8, Christ's bride is ready for the wedding. She is arrayed in "fine linen, bright and clean" (verse 8). Her clothing contrasts sharply with the lavish purple and scarlet dress adorning the prostitute Babylon (Revelation 17:4). God's people have kept themselves undefiled from the impurity of Babylon and are totally faithful to Christ. Now they partake in the Lamb's wedding supper.

The clothing of Christ's bride represents "the righteous deeds of the saints" (Revelation 19:8). This does not mean, however, that God's people are to wear their own deeds. The text states that the bride "was given" bright and clean linen to dress in, representing the righteous deeds (verse 8). Elsewhere in Revelation, Christ supplies the robes of God's people (Revelation 3:18; 6:11), which are washed in the Lamb's blood (Revelation 7:14; 22:14).

The bride readying herself illustrates both the human responsibility and the divine activity in human lives. Paul points to the relationship between the two: "Work out your salvation with fear and trembling; for it is God who is at work in you, both to will and to work for His good pleasure" (Philippians 2:12, 13, NASB). The righteous deeds of God's people are the result of divine activity in their lives (Isaiah 61:10).

At this point, it is important to remember that Revelation 19 does not describe the actual wedding of the Lamb; it only announces that the time for the long-awaited event has finally arrived. The wedding event will take place when God's people are in the New Jerusalem, referred to as "the bride, the wife of the Lamb" (Revelation 21:9). The New Jerusalem and God's people are equated because in that city God's people will finally unite with their Lord for eternity.

Armageddon ends

Back on earth, the time has come for the satanic confederacy to receive its deserved justice. John sees an angel calling in a loud voice to the scavengers of the sky, gathering them together to eat the flesh of the earth's armies, "the great supper of God" (Revelation 19:17). This sharply contrasts with the previous invitation to the Lamb's wedding supper (verse 9). Those called to the Lamb's wedding supper are blessed, while the unrepentant are threatened with becoming the gruesome supper of these birds. The readers of Revelation are offered a choice: either accept the invitation to the Lamb's wedding supper, or be among Christ's opponents, who will be eaten by scavengers.

The scavengers' menu includes people of every sociopolitical level—kings, commanders of one thousand troops, strong people, horses with their horsemen, freemen, slaves—the small and the great (verse 18). All these people received the mark of the beast (Revelation 13:16) and sided with Babylon in the final battle. They are portrayed in the sixth seal scene as "the kings of the earth and the magistrates and the military commanders and the rich and the powerful and every slave and free person" who are trying to hide from God and the Lamb (Revelation 6:15–17). The parallel between the two passages shows that the destruction of the wicked occurs in the context of the Second Coming.

John now sees the worldwide confederacy of political powers fighting Christ and His saints (Revelation 19:19). At that point, Christ appears, completely overthrowing the worldwide confederacy. His coming in glory and power destroys the political confederacy. Revelation 6:15–17 shows the kings and mighty men running in panic, trying to hide from the Lamb's wrath. Furthermore, two members of the satanic triumvirate— the sea beast and the earth beast—are captured and thrown into the lake of fire (Revelation 19:20). The lake of fire is not

an everlasting burning hell but a description of the earth as it
is destroyed by fire. Here will be an ultimate end to rebellion
against God—the same as in Revelation 20:14.

The rest of the people are killed with the sword proceeding
from Christ's mouth. As Paul states, they are destroyed by the
glory of Christ's power (2 Thessalonians 1:8–10). The whole
earth now resembles a battlefield, filled with dead bodies. This
awful scene concludes with the statement that "all the birds were
filled with their flesh" (Revelation 19:21). The defeat of the
rebellion's worldwide confederacy will be final and complete.

The description of the battle of Armageddon, begun in
Revelation 16, is now complete. Babylon is overthrown when
Satan's two allies are cast into the lake of fire. Those who supported Babylon are slain and await the final judgment. The
only one left on earth is Satan, who is awaiting his fate as
described in Revelation 20.

The millennium (20:1-10)
The battle of Armageddon results in the desolation and depopu-
lation of the earth. The destructive winds of the seven last
plagues have caused much destruction, turning the earth into
a barren desert (Revelation 7:1). As Ellen G. White describes it,
the whole earth will look like "a desolate wilderness. The ruins
of cities and villages destroyed by the earthquake, uprooted
trees, ragged rocks thrown out by the sea or torn out of the
earth itself, are scattered over its surface, while vast caverns
mark the spot where the mountains have been rent from their
foundations."[1] The coming of Christ brings the destruction of
the wicked, and their bodies cover the whole earth. The condition of the earth is much like the earth in its chaotic form
before Creation (cf. Genesis 1:2). In such a state, this planet
becomes the place of Satan's imprisonment during the one
thousand years, until he receives his final punishment in the
lake of fire (Revelation 20:10).

Meanwhile, the glorified saints sit on thrones and are authorized to judge. Although the text does not explicitly state where
the resurrected redeemed are during the millennium, Revelation

7:9–17 and 19:1–10 show that they are in heaven. Earlier, John used language that corresponds to Hebrew wedding customs to describe Jesus' return to the earth (Revelation 19:7–9). After betrothing His bride, He returned to His Father's house in heaven to prepare a place for His people. After preparing this place, Christ will come back to take His people to their heavenly home (John 14:3). Peter also talks about the imperishable inheritance reserved for God's people in heaven (see 1 Peter 1:4). All this shows that God's people will spend the millennium in the heavenly place prepared for them by Christ.

The judgment exercised by the saints during the millennium has to do with the question Satan raised at the beginning of the great controversy regarding the fairness of God's actions in the universe. From the beginning, Satan has cultivated doubts concerning God's character and His dealings with humankind. During the process, God will "bring to light the things hidden in the darkness and disclose the motives of men's hearts" (1 Corinthians 4:5, NASB). The redeemed saints are also able to find answers to questions dealing with God's leading in their own lives on earth.

The new earth (21:1-8)

The description of the new world in Revelation 21–22 is given in the language of Genesis 1–3. "In the beginning God created the heavens and the earth" (Genesis 1:1, NASB). On the newly created earth, God gave Adam and Eve the Garden of Eden. With the arrival of sin, however, Eden was lost. The earth became subject to corruption and decay (Romans 8:19–22). Pain, tears, and death took the place of joy, happiness, and life.

But God promised He would "create new heavens and a new earth; and the former things will not be remembered or come to mind" (Isaiah 65:17, NASB). In Revelation 21–22, this promise is fulfilled when God restores the Garden of Eden. All that was lost because of sin is now restored through Jesus Christ. In such a way, God's original plan for the human race is finally realized.

God's presence guarantees a life free of pain and death for

His people on the restored earth. With the destruction of sin, God's presence among His people on earth has been restored. This presence is realized with the New Jerusalem "coming down out of heaven from God" (Revelation 21:2). The descent of the Holy City occurs at the end of the millennium (Revelation 20:7–9). The fact that it comes from heaven shows that the city is not a rebuilt Jerusalem in Palestine, but a heavenly city designed and constructed by God (Hebrews 11:10).

There is no temple in the New Jerusalem because the presence of God makes the city the temple of the new earth (Revelation 21:22). The temple symbolized God's presence among His people (Exodus 25:8; 29:45; Leviticus 26:11, 12); but because of Israel's unfaithfulness, God removed His presence from them (Matthew 23:37, 38). Nonetheless, God promised He would once again make His dwelling place with His people and be their God, and they would be His people (see Ezekiel 37:27). The New Jerusalem does not need a symbol of God's presence because His presence will be real in the city.

God's abiding presence defines the life of His people on the new earth. Revelation describes life on the new earth in terms of what will be absent: no more tears, death, sorrow, crying, and pain (Revelation 21:4; cf. Revelation 7:15–17). All these are the consequences of sin, which no longer exist, for "the first things have passed away" (Revelation 21:4).

At this point, there is a proclamation from God's throne: "Behold, I am making all things new" (verse 5). This declaration is affirmed with the statement that "these words are faithful and true" (verse 5). They are as faithful and true as God is faithful and true. The promise of a life free from sin and suffering comes from God, who is "the Alpha and the Omega, the first and the last, the beginning and the end." This claim begins and concludes the book (Revelation 1:8; 22:13). As God, in the beginning, made the world out of nothing, so at the end of history, He restores it to its original state.

The exterior of the New Jerusalem (21:10-21a)

The reference to "a great and high mountain" (Revelation

21:10) suggests, figuratively speaking, that everything about the new Jerusalem transcends Babylon. Rebuilding a city on the mound of a previously destroyed city was a well-known practice in ancient times (Joshua 11:13; Jeremiah 30:18).[2] This scene appears to affirm God's ultimate triumph over the end-time apostate system (see Isaiah 2:2).

The city radiates the glory of God and appears to John as a jasper stone sparkling like crystal (Revelation 21:11). The New Jerusalem is surrounded by a high wall with three gates on each of the four sides and angels by them (verses 12, 13; cf. Ezekiel 40:5; 48:30–35). The gates on each side allow entry from any direction. Jesus foretold that many would come from the east, west, north, and south and sit at the table in God's kingdom (see Luke 13:29). This prediction is fulfilled in the New Jerusalem, where everyone has unlimited access to God's presence.

The gates of the New Jerusalem are made of huge pearls (Revelation 21:21). As in Ezekiel's vision (Ezekiel 48:30–35), the names of the twelve tribes of Israel are inscribed on them (Revelation 21:12). The New Jerusalem has twelve foundations, decorated with precious stones, similar to the breastplate of the high priest (Exodus 28:17–20). But these stones have the names of the twelve apostles engraved on them, instead of the twelve tribes. This combination symbolizes the union and solidarity of God's Old and New Testament people in the New Jerusalem.

Significantly, the New Jerusalem's cube shape matches the cube shape of the Holy of Holies in the Old Testament temple (1 Kings 6:20). In the earthly temple, the Holy of Holies housed the ark of the covenant, which represented God's throne. The throne of God and of the Lamb is located in the New Jerusalem (Revelation 22:3). Jeremiah prophesied that, in the Messianic age, people would not talk about the ark of the covenant because Jerusalem would be called "the throne of the LORD" (Jeremiah 3:17, NASB). In the earthly temple, only the high priest was allowed to enter the Holy of Holies to meet God; but in the New Jerusalem, this privilege is granted to all the redeemed (Revelation 22:3, 4).

The Book of Revelation

Inside the city (21:21b-22:5)

The Holy City vision concludes with a river of life, flowing from the throne of God and the Lamb (Revelation 22:1). This is reminiscent of the river flowing from Eden, watering the Garden and making it fruitful (Genesis 2:10). The Old Testament prophets often spoke of the river of living waters flowing from the restored temple in Jerusalem and giving life to all (Ezekiel 47:1–12; Joel 3:18; Zechariah 14:8).

On the banks of the river is the tree of life (Revelation 22:2). The tree of life symbolizes eternal life (Genesis 3:22). Because of the curse caused by sin, humans lost access to the tree of life in the Garden of Eden and became subject to death (verses 22–24). Now the redeemed once again have access to the tree of life and share the gift of eternal life that Adam enjoyed prior to the entrance of sin (Revelation 22:3).

The tree of life yields fruit every month, and its leaves are for "the healing of the nations" (verse 2). The New Jerusalem is inhabited by people of all nations, tribes, and languages (Revelation 7:9), just as Zechariah prophesied: "Many nations will join themselves to the LORD in that day and will become My people" (Zechariah 2:11, NASB). All the barriers that separated nations are removed. The curative leaves on the tree of life heal the wounds caused by national, racial, linguistic, and social barriers that have divided people.

> Nation will not lift up sword against nation,
> And never again will they train for war.
> Each of them will sit under his vine
> And under his fig tree,
> With no one to make them afraid (Micah 4:3, 4, NASB).

On the banks of the river of life, each person invites "his neighbor to sit" under the tree of life (Zechariah 3:10, NASB). The redeemed on the restored earth are now one people, belonging to the one great family of God.

In the New Jerusalem, there is no longer any curse (see

Revelation 22:3). Because of the curse that sin brought upon the world, humans were banished from the Garden of Eden. With the eradication of sin, God's people are brought back to the restored Eden. Zechariah prophesied, "People will live in it, and there will no longer be a curse, for Jerusalem will dwell in security" (Zechariah 14:11, NASB).

The greatest of all the privileges the redeemed will enjoy in the New Jerusalem is seeing God face to face (Revelation 22:4), just as Adam did before sin. The perennial desire of humans throughout history has been to see God's face, something that even Moses was denied (Exodus 33:18–20). This is now fulfilled in the New Jerusalem. The redeemed see God as He is (1 John 3:2). They serve Him and worship Him in His temple (see Revelation 7:15). His name is on their foreheads as the reward for refusing the mark of the beast (Revelation 14:1; 15:2). The conclusion of the great controversy marks the beginning of their intimate fellowship with God. "And they will reign forever and ever" (Revelation 22:5).

The book of Revelation closes with a benediction: "The grace of the Lord Jesus be with all" (verse 21). This phrase is more than just a customary benediction. It is God's assurance that people's only hope is in Christ's grace. Christ is the answer to all human hopes and longings amid the enigmas and uncertainties of life. The future may look frightening and gloomy, but God will be with His people until the very end (Matthew 28:20). He holds the future in His hands. His grace is promised to all who take the messages of the Apocalypse seriously, and He will equip His people to endure the tumultuous times of the final crisis. It is through Christ's grace that Revelation's promises become reality. Soon He will return, claim His faithful people, and usher them into their eternal home.

---

1. Ellen G. White, *The Great Controversy* (Nampa, ID: Pacific Press®, 2005), 657.

2. Roberto Badenas, "New Jerusalem—the Holy City," in *Symposium on Revelation—Book 2*, ed. Frank B. Holbrook, Daniel and Revelation Committee Series 7 (Silver Spring, MD: Biblical Research Institute, 1992), 255.